UNVEILING ARIZONA'S ILLUSION: YOUR ADVENTURE GUIDE TO 7 UNIQUE DESTINATIONS

STARGAZE, HIKE, AND CREATE MEMORIES BEYOND THE GRAND CANYON. ESCAPE THE CROWDS AND PLAN YOUR ADVENTURE TODAY WITH THIS EXPERT GUIDE!

CHRISTINA LEAN

TABLE OF CONTENTS

CREATED BY

Christina Lean

For my family, my kids, and all those who have an undefined need to travel, explore, and discover!

INTRODUCTION

Nowhere on this planet is the desert as fascinating as it is in Arizona. –Joseph Stacey

My dearest Arizona,

There is so much to be thankful for when I think of you. You have taught me the beauty of simplicity. Of quiet and minimalism, and peace. You have taught me the value of having a place to call home, a place where I used to take my children exploring. You have shown me that you do not have to go abroad to find adventure and that the most spectacular views are often found in your own backyard.

Thanks to you, I now know that not all deserts look the same, and not all cacti stand as tall and proud as the saguaro. With you, I have seen breathtaking sunsets and magnificent starry skies. You are a testament to the old and the new. Old, abandoned mining towns remind us of your origins. And, while they may no longer have inhabitants, you have endured.

You remain as constant as the red desert sand and rocky mountains through hardship and prosperity. You are not always easy to live with. And yet so much life flourishes within you, Sonoran desert. You have taught me so much in so little time, and I am eternally grateful that I now get to share that knowledge with my children and readers.

Thank you for all you have done for me, Arizona. I will always love you.

When thinking of Arizona, most people get stuck on one thought—the Grand Canyon. And while the Grand Canyon is incredible and a must-see when visiting the state, there are plenty of other gems to see and experience in Arizona. As a native Arizonan and mother, I have acquired years of knowledge and experience with what Arizona offers.

And I believe it is now time to share that knowledge with others who wish to travel to Arizona and experience the peace and beauty of the desert with me.

Whether you are a single exploring the country, charged with planning your next family trip, or looking for a place to go and reconnect with nature, Arizona has something for everyone to enjoy. In addition, Arizona is the perfect place for those feeling overwhelmed to heal and rest.

In a world set on being fast-paced and modern, there is something inspiring about the timelessness of Arizona. It is the perfect place to recharge and take a break from city life without feeling like you are abandoned in the wild. And I am not the only person who feels this way. "Many celebrities, like author Stephanie Meyer, Olympic swimmer Michael Phelps, and actor Asher Angel call Arizona home" (Robinson, 2021).

In this guide, you will learn about the best places to visit and things to do when coming to the state of Arizona. So, whether you enjoy going on hikes, want to visit adventure theme parks, or prefer a cultural holiday packed with museums and history, you will find precisely what you are looking for.

When visiting other states or counties, I have found that it is difficult to find a comprehensive guide to what is available in that area. I always worry that there is something spectacular I am missing out on due to a lack of information. Some locations boast so many attractions that it is difficult to pinpoint which ones are the best. On the contrary, there is so little information about other locations that one might consider skipping it entirely.

I know that I am not alone in this struggle. So, when people want to visit Arizona, I want them to have all the relevant information about the state without the fuss. No more shuffling through thousands of blog posts or forums to select a few attractions. No more worrying if you are missing out on anything spectacular.

Instead, you will get an in-depth discussion of some of the best places to visit in Arizona, including:

- Flagstaff: one of the best areas for seeing Arizona's natural beauty.

- Williams: offers a bit of everything, including natural and manmade attractions.
- Jerome: a city with an interesting and haunting past.
- Page: a city that offers one of Arizona's most impressive architectural projects.
- Phoenix: has one of the best hiking trails in Arizona. It also boasts some exciting tourist attractions for those interested in learning more about the state.
- Sedona: blessed with plenty of natural beauty and attractions for adventurers.
- Tucson: another excellent location for adventurers and thrill seekers.

I will share the history of these seven cities with you, why you should visit these places, and what there is to do and see in each one. Furthermore, I will share an ideal itinerary so that you can plan the perfect day trip to each city. This way, you will have a clear guide of where to go and why. I have always had a deep seeded love for traveling and exploring my beautiful home. After having children, I decided that sharing this love of traveling with them was crucial. However, this was only possible when returning home because life happens, especially in a military family. We were not always located in Arizona.

Ever since they were young, we have visited as many of the tourist attractions and sights in Arizona as possible. My children, therefore, grew up knowing how privileged they are to visit the beautiful state of Arizona and how much there is to see and explore.

And over the years, I have realized that many people don't know about these hidden gems in Arizona. When they think of Arizona, they think of a one-day trip to the Grand Canyon. But Arizona is much bigger than this one attraction—literally!

There is so much to do, see, and experience that I felt it was my duty, and honor, to share all that I have learned about the state so you, too, can enjoy this wonderful place.

Because Arizona is so diverse, you can see many things here. If you prefer being close to the city, there are plenty of large cities and towns with some of the best universities in the country.

If you prefer being surrounded by undisturbed nature, there are countless hiking trails and camping locations for you to stay at. And, if your family or friends are thrill seekers, there are also a few theme parks worth visiting.

Arizona is the perfect place to escape, whether you have an entire week or only a short weekend. So, what are you waiting for? Let's delve into the details and explore the fantastic places and things Arizona has to offer.

1

FLAGSTAFF

In the empire of the desert, water is the king, and shadow is the queen. –Mehmet Murat İldan

The first stop in this guide to Arizona is in Flagstaff. Flagstaff is one of the first towns you come across when leaving the Grand Canyon, which is why it has become a popular stop for thirsty tourists. But that is not all Flagstaff is good for. On the contrary, Flagstaff offers plenty of natural wonder and activities for every adventurer who passes through.

But before I explain what you should do and see in Flagstaff, let me first explain how Flagstaff came to be.

A Little Bit of History

To understand Flagstaff's importance and significance, you must first understand its history. Flagstaff was founded as a town in 1876 ("Flagstaff Arizona," n.d.) and was already an essential stop. In addition, Flagstaff is located near a spring, which was crucial in the desert. This made it an essential pit stop on the way from Albuquerque to California.

Due to eruptions of the Sunset Crater years ago, the Flagstaff area had rich soil. The fertile soil and springs made Flagstaff a crucial stop along the wagon road and the later railroad to get water and supplies.

Long before the town was known as Flagstaff, when there was nothing but open grasslands, the Sinagua people lived there. They were primarily hunter-gatherers and farmers who cultivated corn where they could. They may have resided near current-day Flagstaff for a while because of the springs there.

However, they left the area long before Western settlers arrived, likely due to a lack of natural resources or disputes with neighboring clans. So, when the first settlers arrived at the springs, they found them void of any people. This event occurred somewhere between 1850 and 1860 ("Flagstaff Arizona," n.d.) when Antoine Leroux and Edward Fitzgerald Beale set out to build a road across Arizona.

They camped near the springs, later called the Leroux Springs, for the night. Legend has it that they stripped one of the trees of its bark and branches and used it as a flagstaff to hoist a flag and signal their presence to those who followed. This is one of the theories of how Flagstaff got its name.

As time passed, more people moved to the area

because of its fertile soil and water source. Soon, a post office opened, and Flagstaff was recognized as a town in 1876. When the railroad reached the town, it developed even further. Many people saw the opportunity to farm cattle and sheep in the area, and the railroad made it possible to transport their goods to the city.

The timber industry was also booming in Flagstaff because of its proximity to what is now known as Coconino National Forest. In 1891, Flagstaff also became the seat of Coconino County, giving this town even more prominence.

But of course, Flagstaff also had its share of problems. The springs did not offer enough water for all the citizens, especially with so many fires and natural disasters tapping the water supplies. And there was also a big gambling and drinking problem in the town during the late 1800s and early 1900s.

But the town still grew as it was an important stop along the railroad from Albuquerque to California. Many people also came to Flagstaff to visit the Grand Canyon, which is less than a mile away.

Flagstaff would become home to Northern Arizona University in 1966 and only continued to grow from there into the city it is today. Today, Flagstaff has an estimated 80,000 residents, according to census reports. It also sees thousands of tourists yearly who flock to the city not only to see the Grand Canyon but also to explore the landmarks and attractions in the city itself. So, what are the attractions Flagstaff has to offer?

Arizona Snowbowl

The first stop in Flagstaff for any adventurer should be Arizona Snowbowl. Arizona Snowbowl is a ski resort and hiking trail that leads to Humphreys Peak, the highest point in Arizona state ("About the Mountain," n.d.). From the peak, you can see the desert mountains of Phoenix, the White Mountains, and even the rim of the Grand Canyon. Although this is a strenuous hike, the view from the top is well worth the effort.

The Arizona Snowbowl hike is found on the western slope of the San Francisco peaks, which is just north of Flagstaff. But of course, for those who don't like hiking, there are also other reasons to visit Arizona Snowbowl. It happens to be one of two exquisite ski resorts in Flagstaff.

So, those who don't enjoy hiking might prefer to bring their ski gear and make a ski trip to the Snowbowl instead. Then, the more experienced skiers can head up the mountain for some extreme fun, while children and beginners also have the opportunity to enjoy themselves.

Bunny Hill and Heart Prairie are perfect for children who want fun but aren't confident on the bigger slopes. Arizona Snowbowl even has a ski school at the resort for first-timers or those who want to sharpen their skiing skills.

When hiking up Humphreys Peak, you will need all the hiking gear you usually need for hiking in snow, including:

- Hiking boots

- A day pack
- Water and food
- Ice picks
- Snow boots with spikes
- Warm clothes

Fortunately, you don't require any specific hiking equipment for the Arizona Snowbowl hike. However, if the weather is unpleasant, the ski resort may close the hiking trail due to safety concerns.

If you want to go skiing at Arizona Snowbowl, you are welcome to bring your ski gear. But you may also rent it from the resort if you don't have any gear. Tickets to ski at Arizona Snowbowl cost between $50 and $100. You can also use the shuttle service to transport you to and from town, which costs around $20 per trip.

Hiking at Arizona Snowbowl is much cheaper, with tickets averaging around $15 per person. Also, budget some additional funds for food and drinks during the day.

There are plenty of places to stay near the Arizona Snowbowl. However, most experienced hikers and skiers recommend staying at Basecamp to ensure you get a spot on the slope, as staff may turn you away if the slope reaches capacity. Fortunately, Basecamp is just a few minutes away from Arizona Snowbowl, which means you can arrive at the resort in time for the opening of the slopes.

Arizona Snowbowl is the perfect stop in Flagstaff when traveling there in winter. It will surely give you a new perspective on Arizona state. I recommend buying your tickets in advance and keeping an eye on the weather forecast before heading there to avoid disappointment. If snowy mountains and hiking isn't your idea of a perfect getaway, fear not! Flagstaff has plenty of other attractions to visit.

Coconino Lava River Cave

Suppose you want to see something truly spectacular and unique while visiting Flagstaff. In that case, you must take a drive to the Coconino lava river cave. This underground cave formed thousands of years ago when a vent at Heart Prairie erupted, and lava flowed down the mountain. As the top and sides of the lava cooled first, it created a closed river through which the rest of the molten rock flowed.

Eventually, everything became solid, leaving behind an underground cave of wonders. On this hike, you can see where the lava flowed, as the entire cave is covered in slick, uneven black rock. The Coconino lava river cave is located 14 miles north of Flagstaff (Martinez, n.d.).

Because it is an underground cave, you will need a few things to do this ¾ mile hike. Forest Services recommend bringing at least three light sources, as pitch black inside the caves and the dark stone walls make it even more challenging to see. Bring a torch, headlight, and backup light source. You'll also need sturdy hiking boots or trail running shoes. The cave floor is slippery and uneven, so you will need supportive and grippy shoes.

If you have an ankle injury, this might not be the best hiking trail. Also, because the cave roof is quite low at some points, consider bringing a helmet if you have one. While it isn't necessary, there is a risk of bumping your head against the roof at lower sections. And, because the visibility inside the cave is so poor, extra protection is always advised.

There aren't any shops or restaurants near the cave, so you should also bring food and water for the hike. Remember to follow the "pack it in, pack it out" rules of hiking, as littering is strictly prohibited at this site. There have been cases of graffiti painted on the cave walls. And although the graffiti has since been removed, it is crucial that you leave the caves exactly how you find them to preserve this unique attraction for future visitors.

While the Coconino Lava River cave is a truly spectacular site, it is unsuitable for people with claustrophobia or children. The cave is completely closed at all sides, so people with claustrophobia may have difficulty on this hike. Furthermore, the entrance to the cave is quite narrow, making it even more daunting for those who don't like enclosed spaces.

If you want to bring your children on the hike, they should be old enough to navigate alone. Poor visibility and uneven floors make bringing strollers or carriers into the cave impossible. If the children are too small to walk alone, they will have much more difficulty scrambling over the boulders at the cave entrance.

Therefore, it is recommended that you save this trip for when your kids are old enough to walk by themselves. You don't need a special permit to access the Coconino lava river cave, and there aren't any fees. This means that you can hike the Coconino lava river cave as often as you like, so you don't have to worry about the kids missing out.

Lowell Observatory

Did you know that one of the first things built in Flagstaff was the observatory? The Lowell Observatory was erected in 1894 by Percival Lowell ("Lowell Observatory Flagstaff," n.d.). Flagstaff was chosen as the location for the observatory because of its clear, unpolluted skies and high altitude. Several important discoveries have been made at Lowell observatory, including the discovery of Pluto and the moon mapping mission for Apollo.

Therefore, one cannot visit Flagstaff without planning a trip to the observatory. While it is open throughout the day, I recommend going at night, because this is when you will have the best views of the stars. There are several telescopes and lookout points to enjoy the spectacular night sky.

There is also an hour-long guided tour, where the highly informed guides share the history of the Lowell Observatory and some of the impressive discoveries made here. The guided tour features a lecture and presentation with stunning images and interactive displays.

You can attend several programs when visiting the Lowell Observatory, including a tour of the Clark telescope, a historical display of the observatory, and science demonstrations related to the stars. Several daytime programs are also available for those who cannot visit the observatory at night.

Of course, everyone comes to the observatory to see the stars, which is why there are several viewing decks with telescopes. The guides will assist you in looking at specific points in the sky. While you will have a magnificent view regardless of when you visit, I recommend planning your trip to the Lowell observatory during the dark moon, as this will give you the best view of the stars.

Book your tickets in advance to ensure a spot for the evening's events. Children of all ages are welcome at the observatory, and the guides are friendly and accommodating toward the children when helping them look through the telescopes. There is also a kids' corner at the observatory, where children can learn more about stars and the observatory.

However, despite being accommodating towards children, young ones may find the lectures on the tour tedious and may become disruptive for other visitors. So, if your children aren't interested in learning about space and they are too young to pay attention or sit still during an hour-long lecture, this might not be the ideal family outing.

You must buy tickets to the observatory, sold online or at the door. Ticket prices are as follows:

- Adults: $29
- College students: $19
- Children (5-17): $17
- AAA members/seniors (55+)/military personnel: $26

You don't need to bring anything special when visiting the observatory. However, dress warmly when going in winter, as you will be spending time outside while looking through the telescopes. The Lowell Observatory is one of the best reasons to visit Flagstaff because it is a testament to the history and scientific advancements made since its founding.

Museum of Northern Arizona

If you want to learn more about the history of Flagstaff and the larger Colorado plateau, make time to visit the Museum of Northern Arizona. The museum offers many relics and artifacts recovered from the area. It is largely dedicated to the Native American tribes who inhabited the area before Western settlers discovered Flagstaff and its surroundings. But the museum also shares some history about the region, including the Grand Canyon, Lava River Cave, Lowell Observatory, and prominent families in Flagstaff's history, like the Riordan family.

The Museum of Northern Arizona itself has a long history. It opened in 1928 and has always been dedicated to sharing information about the area and its inhabitants. You can buy tickets at the door or schedule a trip to the museum in advance. This lets you schedule your trip there when the museum isn't as crowded.

I recommend planning your trip to the museum before any other activities, as there is a lot of historical and interesting information about all the attractions around Flagstaff. The museum serves as an introduction to Flagstaff and will give you a better understanding of all the other sites in and around town.

You can learn about the Native American tribes who lived in the area before the Western settlers. Evidence of their presence is clear in the museum thanks to the many artifacts recovered from the region. Furthermore, you will get a great history lesson about Flagstaff in general, including how the town was founded, which industries initially thrived in the area, and what challenges Flagstaff faced over the years.

The Museum of Northern Arizona caters to families, so special programs exist for children. You can collect an activity booklet for your children at the front desk to keep them entertained while you tour the museum. Furthermore, there is a Discovery corner where children can play and relax when they get bored inside the museum.

There are also plenty of interactive artifacts throughout the museum that children can touch. This allows them to engage all their senses for a better experience. And you can take the children for a stroll outside on the museum grounds if they get agitated from being inside for too long.

You don't need any special equipment to visit the Museum of Northern Arizona. While you may bring water in, no food is allowed inside. But you can have a picnic outside after exploring the museum.

Tickets are for sale online or at the door. Children under nine may enter the museum for free. Ticket prices are as follows:

- Adults: $15
- Children (10-17): $10
- Native Americans (from age 10): $10

The museum has special events at times. I recommend consulting their website before going, so you know what the schedule will look like when you visit. The Museum of Northern Arizona is one of Flagstaff's most popular tourist attractions, and many people visit the city, especially to see the artifacts there.

Riordan Mansion State Historic Park

If you are more interested in learning about the history of Flagstaff and the prominent families who ensured its success, plan a trip to Riordan Mansion State National Park. While this area is now a national state park, it was once the private lodgings of the Riordan family.

Built in 1904 by Timothy and Michael Riordan, the Riordan Mansion is a celebration of the flourishing lumber industry in Flagstaff at the time ("Riordan Mansion," 2022). The Riordan family was responsible for much of the lumber industry in Flagstaff, and they were prominent community members at the time. Their estate is a proclamation of their wealth and social standing. The mansion has 40 rooms, and the estate covers 13,000 square feet.

If you aren't too interested in the family's history, you can visit the estate at no cost and take a self-guided tour. While you cannot enter the mansion, you may take a walk on the park grounds, enjoy a packed lunch on the park benches, and enjoy the splendid surroundings of the mansion.

However, suppose you want to learn more about the Riordan family and their place in Flagstaff's history. In that case, a guided tour is also available at a cost. Children under six can take the tour for free, while children between seven and thirteen pay $7 for a ticket. Adults pay $12. The tour is about an hour long and takes you through the mansion and into the garages, where a display of the family history is kept.

You can visit the arts and crafts corner and gift shop, which is also located in the garage, while on the tour. You will learn about the family, their activities, and their importance in Flagstaff. Although the guided tour is ideal for history buffs and adults, it might be tedious for children. You may not bring any strollers or large carriers on the guided tour, meaning this tour isn't ideal for small children.

Fortunately, there is also an excellent activity, especially for the young ones. If your children are between six and twelve, you can enroll them in the junior ranger program at Riordan Mansion State Historic Park ("Riordan Mansion State," 2022). Download the junior ranger form and fill it in before going to the park.

Then, enquire about the information booklet and activities for the kids when you arrive at the park. They will get assignments to complete at the park, be sworn in as junior rangers, and receive ranger buttons. This is a free activity for the kids to enjoy and is available at most state parks in Arizona. This allows them to collect junior ranger badges as you travel through the state, adding to the fun and memories while there.

Riordan Mansion State Historic Park is an excellent destination in Flagstaff for families and those interested in the town's history. It is also the ideal spot for those interested in architecture, as the mansion is beautifully built with local materials, such as timber from the surrounding forests and volcanic stone arches from the sunset crater volcano.

Route 66

Route 66 is likely one of the most famous routes in Arizona. It started as a wagon road in the 1850s and later became a railroad connecting all of Arizona. Over the years, Route 66 has been changed and split many times, but parts of the original route are still visible if you know where to look. And you can find part of the original Route 66 road in Flagstaff.

Also known as "The Mother Road" (Wittig, n.d.), Route 66 was crucial in developing Flagstaff from a small railroad stop to its current city. And as you can imagine, there are many interesting stops along Route 66. The section of the road running through Flagstaff is no exception.

One of the most interactive things on Route 66 is gathering stamps for the secret Route 66 passport. You can find more information about this passport online. Essentially, it is a secret book you can get stamped at specific locations along Route 66. It makes for an excellent souvenir of your time in Arizona and a great activity with kids.

Another fun activity to do on Route 66 in Flagstaff is to take a self-guided walking tour. An audio tour book named *Walk This Talk* (2020) is an informative audio guide that takes you through Route 66 in Flagstaff. It explains the history of the route and gives great recommendations of places to stop and see along the route. This is an excellent activity for the family or anyone who enjoys walking and wants to discover downtown Flagstaff.

Of course, there are also many restaurants and quaint antique shops located along Route 66, making it the perfect way to spend a day getting to know what Flagstaff was once like. Don't forget to take a picture at the Route 66 mural on Phoenix Avenue or stop by the Mother Road Brewing Company for beer and a historical experience of the old Flagstaff.

There aren't any costs associated with visiting Route 66 in Flagstaff. However, you should still budget some money for stopping at some restaurants and buying some Route 66 trinkets while there.

Although Route 66 isn't a specific attraction like some others, many tourists visit Flagstaff yearly to see what Arizonan towns were like in the late 1800s and early 1900s. Because Route 66 plays such an important role in the development of Flagstaff and the state of Arizona, it would be a shame to pass up on the opportunity to explore this route while in the city.

Sunset Crater Volcano

When learning about the history of Flagstaff, you may notice that many historical accounts mention the Sunset Crater Volcano eruption as the cause of the uncanny fertile soil found around Flagstaff. The volcanic ash that mixed with the soil after the eruption caused the soil to be as fertile as it is. This initially led people to settle in the area, and they eventually developed it into the city of Flagstaff.

Suffice it to say that the Sunset Crater Volcano plays an important part in the history and success of Flagstaff. Today, you can visit the Sunset Crater Volcano and hike one of the many trails around the crater.

Unfortunately, in 2022, a massive wildfire destroyed many parts of the Sunset Crater Volcano hiking trails and visitor center. But as the centers are rebuilt, and nature restores itself, the park will slowly reopen again for visitors. Once fully open, one can do many exciting things at the Sunset Crater Volcano.

Several fantastic hiking trails vary in length and difficulty are found at Sunset Crater Volcano. However, most of the trails are considered easy and are, therefore, kid-friendly too. "The Paved Lava Flow Trail and A'Ah Lava Trails are some of the park's easiest and most kid-friendly trails" (Fromm, 2022).

There is also an insightful visitor center where you can learn more about the history of the Sunset Crater Volcano, when it last erupted, and how the lava flowed when this eruption occurred. The visitor center is also child friendly, with lectures about volcanoes and lava for children and adults to attend.

Be sure to consult the Sunset Crater Volcano Park website before visiting to see if there are any special lectures or activities. These activities are often held on park grounds, including special guest visitors discussing the area and the volcano's history.

Like Riordan Mansion State Historic Park, Sunset Crater Volcano Park also has a junior ranger program. Children between six and twelve can download and fill in the activity chart and receive a Sunset Crater Volcano junior ranger badge. Some of the activities in the book include taking a hike on one of the trails and interviewing a park ranger. This allows children to explore the park and learn more about being park rangers.

The park staff puts a lot of effort into ensuring something for everyone at Sunset Crater Volcano. The views are spectacular, especially at sunset, which is another reason you should visit the park. There are also many birds and small animals to see at the park, so remember to pack your binoculars.

You require a park entry pass to visit Sunset Crater Volcano. The pass is $25 for a private vehicle and is valid for seven days, giving you plenty of time to visit the park and complete multiple hiking trails. You can also purchase a Flagstaff Area National Monuments pass, which grants you access to Sunset Crater Volcano Park and other parks around Flagstaff.

Walnut Canyon National Monument

The Walnut Canyon National Monument offers a unique experience. Walnut Canyon is so named because of Walnut Creek that eroded the rock surfaces to form the canyon over thousands of years. Today, Walnut Canyon National Monument is a state park. It has a visitor center, museum, and several interesting hiking trails.

This park offers a mixture of natural scenery and history lessons. At the visitor center, you can learn more about the Sinagua people who lived in Walnut Canyon and the surrounding areas hundreds of years ago. You will also see some artifacts recovered from their homes' remains in the park at the visitor center.

Of course, the most popular thing to do at Walnut Canyon, and the primary reason people visit the park, is to hike into the Canyon. Several hiking trails take you past some of the ruins of the Sinagua people who lived there. These ruins include homes and grain stores. You can see them scattered across the Canyon. Most of these buildings were built using sandstone, clay, and wooden pillars. They are built in the caves and alcoves of Walnut Canyon, with the cave tops serving as the roof.

You may also notice the pit houses located on the canyon rim where grain and other harvested food were stored. Many of the Sinagua ruins are well preserved, and you may actually enter some of them too. Inside, you will see the "blackened walls created by the fires made to keep people warm and cook food" (Fromm, 2020).

The trails also give you a spectacular view of the

Canyon. The diverse plant-and-animal life is another factor that makes Walnut Canyon such a unique experience. You will see firsthand what I mean when you see also the plants that grow in the Canyon.

Most of the hiking trails at Walnut Canyon are rated as easy to moderate in difficulty. The most popular trails are the Walnut Canyon Island trail and the Walnut Canyon Rim and Ruins Loop. The Island trail is paved with many steps and benches for resting. Although the descent into the Canyon is quite steep, this trail is easy enough for children to complete. Unfortunately, because of its steepness, you won't be able to bring a stroller or carrier on the hike.

Like many other state parks in Flagstaff, Walnut Canyon National Monument offers a junior ranger program. This program is designed for children between the ages of six and twelve. You can collect a junior ranger booklet at the visitor center. Once completed, children will receive a Walnut Canyon junior ranger badge.

You require a pass to enter Walnut Canyon. This pass can be ordered online in advance and is $25 per vehicle. The pass is valid for seven days, giving you more than enough time to explore Walnut Canyon and stop at the visitor center and museum.

Wupatki National Monument

Suppose you are in Flagstaff and want to go on a cultural excursion or road trip; Wupatki National Monument is the place to go.

The Wupatki National Monument is about 30 miles

north of Flagstaff. It shows an incredible display of Pueblos that belonged to the Sinagua people who inhabited the area hundreds of years ago. They were farmers who cultivated corn, legumes, and squashes in the area. Given how fertile the soil was after the eruption of the Sunset Crater volcano, many Sinagua people relocated here. This is why there are so many structures at the Wupatki site.

The Wupatki National Monument was founded in 1924 and covers an area of 55 square feet. There are more than 30 buildings and structures on this piece of land, making it an impressive attraction to visit.

"When visiting the monument, you will see many structures built between the 11th and 13th centuries by the Sinagua people and other tribes" ("Wupatki National Monument Brittanica," 2013). These pueblos are mostly single-story or double-story houses with single rooms. However, there are also larger buildings, including an amphitheater and ball court. Because these structures were constructed with red sandstone and mortar, most still stand and are in excellent condition.

And what's even more impressive are the artifacts recovered from the structures before the monument opened. Items such as shell bracelets and pottery suggest that the Sinagua people traded with other clans, which is likely how they thrived in such a harsh environment.

Most of the recovered artifacts are kept on display at the visitor center or the Museum of Northern Arizona. The best way to see these impressive structures is by hiking on one of the many trails that lead past them.

All trails are rated as easy, and some are even wheelchair accessible. Because of the ease of these trails, they are also child friendly. And, considering that the trails are paved, you can also bring a stroller or carrier on the hike. Most trails are loops of 0.2 to 0.5 miles. Because the hikes are so short and easy, Wupatki National Monument makes an excellent family outing for anyone with children or senior citizens in their group.

Children can also complete the junior ranger course at Wupatki National Monument. You can enquire about this project at the visitor center. After completing the booklet activities, children may receive a junior ranger badge. They can collect multiple badges at various state parks and monuments in Arizona. Suppose you want more excitement at Wupatki National Monument. In that case, you can also sign up for a guided overnight hike.

These hikes aren't open to all guests and must be arranged in advance. You can only sign up for one of them from November to March. There are different hikes, ranging from moderate to extremely strenuous in difficulty. "Each hike explores a unique part of the monument. For example, the Crack-in-Rock overnight hike takes you to some Sinagua rock paintings" ("Wupatki National Monument," n.d.).

You need a permit to access the Wupatki National Monument. You can purchase it online before arrival, priced at $25 per vehicle. This permit is valid for 7 days so that you can visit the monument multiple times. Other permits grant you access to multiple state parks and monuments around Flagstaff.

A Day in Flagstaff

Although there are so many wonderful things to do in Flagstaff, Arizona, you might wonder what you should do if you only have limited time there. For example, what should you do if you only have a day in Flagstaff?

Unfortunately, you cannot do everything mentioned above in only one day. But there are several things you can do. So, here is my perfect itinerary for a day in Flagstaff.

Take a day hike

As you have noticed, one of the most popular activities in Flagstaff is hiking. Whether hiking up Humphrey's Peak or into Walnut Canyon to see the Sinagua ruins, you will likely do some hiking while in Flagstaff. It is truly one of the best ways to explore the area.

With limited time, choose one of the shorter trails around the city, especially when hiking with children. Some hikes to consider include:

- The Island trail at Walnut Canyon
- The Lava River Cave trial
- The A'Ah Lava trail at Sunset Crater Volcano
- The self-guided tour of Route 66

Try doing the hike early in the day so you can enjoy the sunrise and still have the rest of the day open for other activities in Flagstaff.

Picnic at Lake Mary

After a morning hike around Flagstaff, there is no better way to enjoy breakfast or an early lunch than with a picnic at Lake Mary (Upper). So, pack a basket with your favorite snacks and food, and enjoy the tranquil silence at the lake. Lake Mary is located 12 miles Southeast of Flagstaff in the Coconino National Forest. The lake is surrounded by green grass and clear skies.

It gives you a sense of the beauty of Flagstaff. This scene is entirely at odds with what people think of when they imagine Arizona, as it is anything but a desert scene. Remember to take all your belongings with you when you leave the lake to preserve its beauty.

Go to the Museum of Northern Arizona

If you want an overview of Flagstaff's history, there is only one place you can go—the Museum of Northern Arizona. Here, you will learn about the Sinagua people who roamed the lands long before it was named Flagstaff. You will also learn about the early history of Flagstaff, how it was founded, and how this town shaped Arizona.

The Museum of Northern Arizona is the perfect place to get an overview of Flagstaff. It has such an impressive interactive display that many people come to Flagstaff primarily to visit the museum.

Visit Lowell Observatory

Once you are done at the museum, your next stop should be the Lowell Observatory. Try to plan your day so that you visit the observatory at night because this is when you will have the best views. The Lowell Observatory is a part of Flagstaff's history. Many important discoveries have been made here, including the discovery of Pluto.

There are many things to see and do at the observatory. I recommend deciding what you want to accomplish at the observatory before going, so you can plan your time accordingly.

Tour and Dinner in Downtown Historic District

Finally, you cannot visit Flagstaff without taking a trip to the downtown historic district and Route 66. A self-guided audio tour of the Route 66 area in Flagstaff will be the perfect way to spend your day. Stop at one of the historic hotels or diners for dinner and get a taste of what Flagstaff was like in the early 1900s.

Flagstaff is a city with a lot of history and natural beauty. It is the ideal family stop in Arizona, and you are guaranteed to have some memorable stories to share after visiting this city.

But Flagstaff is not the only city you should visit in Arizona. Arizona has several other important stops, including the next city in this guide, Williams.

2

WILLIAMS

For all the toll the desert takes on a man, it gives compensation,
deep breaths, deep sleep, and the communion of the stars. –
Mary Austin

If your next destination on your trip through Arizona is Williams, you're in luck! There is something so wonderful about this small town that this guide would not be complete without mentioning it. Williams has around 4,000 permanent residents, but most of its income comes from the thousands, if not millions, of tourists who visit it annually on their way to the Grand Canyon. I loved camping around Williams!

Williams is home to the Southern terminal of the Grand Canyon Railway. Many people board the train here and head for Grand Canyon Village. But it served another purpose before Williams became a popular pit stop for tourists wanting to see this natural wonder. To understand

Williams's current circumstances, you must first understand its history.

A Little Bit of History

Williams' history dates back to 1864 when the area was selected as the Atlantic and Pacific Railroad location. "Some settlers had already arrived in the area before 1864, the first recorded people being Sam Ball, John Vitnon, and T.C. Rogers" (Howell, 2016). T.C. Rogers saw to the arrival of a post office in Williams in 1881. The town was incorporated in 1901.

The town was named after William S. Williams, also known as Old Bill Williams. He was a prominent trapper and mountain man frequently seen trapping beavers between 1826 and 1869. The surrounding mountains are also named after him. "You can see a statue of Old Bill Williams in the south of town" (Speakman, 2020).

After T.C. bought out Ball and Winton and became the first official settler in the area, other permanent residents followed. Many were ranchers and farmers who produced food to transport on the railway. When the railway began, many more people moved to Williams to help build the Atlantic and Pacific railway when construction on the railway began. Another contributing factor to the increased population in Williams was the lumber sector. In 1882, the first lumber Mill, Wilson, and Haskel Lumber Mill, was built in Williams. The lumber mill produced lumber for the railroad, and many people came to Williams to work at the mill. By 1894, at least three lumber mills were located around Williams, all bringing new settlers and job opportunities to town. As such, Williams' population grew, and in 1882 the first school opened in town. It had 23 pupils at the time. By 1906, the school had 160 students, and an official school building was erected.

Williams continued to grow until 1984, when Interstate 40 was completed and the previous main road, Route 66, was discontinued. Interstate 40 runs around Williams instead of going through it, like Route 66. Like many other towns that used to be on the main road through Arizona, Williams' financial and population and financial growth took a hard hit after the completion of Interstate 40. Fortunately, because the Grand Canyon Railway still runs from Williams, tourists continued to visit the town.

Today, Williams' primary source of income is the tourists who visit, and you will see many diners, pubs, and hotels in town because of it. In addition, downtown Williams and the remainder of Route 66 are registered as Historic Sites, further drawing tourists to town. So, what can one do and see in Williams when visiting today? Continue reading to find out!

Raptor Ranch Birds of Prey

Raptor Ranch Birds of Prey is a must-see for anyone interested in birds of prey, dinosaurs, or the Grand Canyon. The ranch offers a fun-filled program for children and adults. You can learn more about the birds of prey in Arizona, visit Bed Rock City, and drive in a Hummer to the Grand Canyon and the surrounding area.

Raptor Ranch Birds of Prey is home to several species of birds, including the Arizona Raptor and several owl species. The ranch hosts daily raptor flight shows where you can see the birds in action. You can also get up close and personal with the birds by holding them. The visitor center and website have more information about bird show times and encounters.

If you are more interested in dinosaurs, why not visit Bed Rock City? Bed Rock City is modeled after The Flintstones, a popular cartoon from the 1990s about a family of cavemen. The city has models of houses, dinosaurs, and fun slides for the kids (and adults) to enjoy. Furthermore, the ranch has a dinosaur exhibit. You can learn more about the history and evidence of dinosaurs in Arizona millions of years ago. There is also an interactive exhibit where you can try your luck at digging for dinosaur bones. This interactive exhibit is great for the kids, but adults are welcome to attend too.

If you want to visit the Grand Canyon, you can also do so at the Raptor Ranch. Here, a specialized guide will take you to the southern rim of the Grand Canyon in a decommissioned military Hummer. You can enjoy the view while learning about the history of the Grand Canyon and the Grand Canyon National Park.

Furthermore, you can learn about hydroponic gardening when visiting the hydroponic garden on the ranch. One of the guides will explain all you need to know about growing vegetables, fruits, and herbs with a hydroponic system. This might just become your new obsession when returning home!

Of course, the ranch also has a visitor center, gift shop, and restaurant. Stop by Fred's Diner for lunch or dinner. When visiting on a Saturday, you can also enjoy some BBQ meat made to order. If one day isn't enough time to explore everything on offer at Raptor Ranch Birds of Prey, you can also camp or stay in the luxury Fifth Wheel Trailer. The park has 30 camping spots suitable for tent camping or RVs. Each campsite has running water, electricity, and access to a bathroom and shower.

Prices for the campsite start at $40, depending on your chosen lot and the size of your camper. Entrance to the Raptor Ranch Birds of Prey is $8. However, campers and residents may enjoy all the amenities for free. As the Raptor Ranch Birds of Prey is only 20 minutes from Grand Canyon National Park, it is a convenient pit stop between the park and Williams.

Sycamore Falls

Sycamore Falls is known to many as "Arizona's best-kept secret" (Young, 2020). Sycamore Falls is an hour and a half from the Grand Canyon, located in the Sycamore Canyon. This canyon has a diverse ecosystem. Toward the top of the mountain, the landscape is covered in pine trees, while the other end of the canyon ends in the desert terrain of the Verde Valley.

There is a lot to see and explore in the Sycamore Canyon. But the reason most people make the journey is to see Sycamore Falls. These waterfalls and water holes are popular tourist destinations. However, many people aren't aware of their existence when visiting Williams. Fortunately, this means you won't cross too many crowds on your way to the falls.

Reaching Sycamore Falls is easy and can be done in several ways. The first way is by driving up through Sycamore Canyon to the Trailhead. It is a short ¾-mile hike from the trailhead to the falls. The first part of the trail is a steep descent with loose rocks. After that, the trail evens out. Finally, you will come to a fork—"the locals also refer to Sycamore Falls as Paradise Forks or the Forks for this reason" (Zahanna, 2022). Taking either fork will lead you to one of the Sycamore Falls.

I recommend visiting both falls. While there isn't always an active waterfall at Sycamore Falls, the view from the top is spectacular, regardless. A large turquoise pool surrounded by sheer drops awaits you at the end of each fork. You may see water trickling down the rocks if you are lucky enough. You are more likely to see the waterfalls in late winter, early spring, or after a summer monsoon.

While most people visit the Sycamore Falls by car, you can also see them as part of the longer, 11-mile rim trail. This is a fantastic hiking trail for those with enough endurance to complete it. Sycamore Falls is only one of the landmarks you will see along the trail. And because the trail isn't too crowded, you will have most of the viewpoints and trail all to yourself.

Hiking the Rim Trail in Sycamore Canyon is not for the faint of heart. You need proper hiking equipment and experience. This trail is rated as moderate to extreme in difficulty. However, the hike from the trailhead is an easy hike that most children can also complete. You cannot bring a stroller, though, as the first section of the trail is steep and uneven.

There are no fees for visiting Sycamore Falls. The best time to go is at sunrise or sunset when you can capture the sun behind the falls. Bring a hat, sunscreen, and comfortable walking shoes when hiking to Sycamore Falls, and always remember the "pack-it-in, pack-it-out" rules of hiking.

Grand Canyon Railway

If you are in Arizona to see the Grand Canyon, there is no better way to reach it than by train. This is how people have been journeying for over 100 years, and Williams offers the best Grand Canyon Experience. The Grand Canyon Railway has been operating from Williams since 1901. It takes passengers to the southern rim of the Grand Canyon. On this two-and-a-half-hour journey from Williams to the Grand Canyon, you will see some of Arizona's most spectacular scenery. The train ride starts you through the pine forest in Williams. As you near the canyon, the environment becomes more and more desert-like.

The train hosts and hostesses make the best of the train ride by sharing information about the train, the Grand Canyon, and Williams. There is a gift shop, dining cart, and observation platform on the train, so you have plenty to keep busy with while making your way to the Canyon. The train also has live musicians and storytellers onboard, so you will surely be entertained.

The Grand Canyon Railway experience is not only for those who want to learn more about the canyon. Instead, it is meant for the entire family. Before boarding the train, watch a live-action Western shootout outside the terminal. The performance is funny, historically accurate, and sets the scene for what's to come. The train terminal resembles what it would have looked like in the 1900s. The terminal has plenty of props to take photos with, and it is large and comfortable.

Once you board the train, you can sit back, relax, and enjoy the ride. The same cast who appeared in the shootout made a second appearance on the train ride. Here, they are train robbers coming to steal your valuables. This part of the train ride is especially entertaining for kids (and adults).

When you reach the historic village at the southern rim of the Grand Canyon, you will depart the train at the historic Grand Canyon Village and get on a bus that takes you to the Grand Canyon viewing deck. The whole experience is truly enjoyable and makes your time in Williams something special. If you want an even more unique experience, why not stay in the Grand Canyon Railway Hotel?

This hotel is conveniently located right next to the terminal. The hotel lobby is built and decorated to remind you of the early 1900s. The rooms are also spacious and comfortable. The hotel has a restaurant serving breakfast and dinner to all visiting guests. Furthermore, it is a short walk from the historic Route 66 and the Williams town center.

You can choose from several packages at the hotel, some offering meals and others including the Grand Canyon Railway experience. Lodging at the hotel starts at $350 per person. Consult the website for special rates and details about the package deals.

The Grand Canyon Railway experience is one that anyone will enjoy. Admission for the train, including the gunfight show and transport to and from the Canyon, is $82 for adults and $51 for children (2-15). Although this experience is more expensive, you will surely remember it forever.

Bearizona Wildlife Park

The Bearizona Wildlife Park is another unique experience you will likely only have once in your lifetime. The park is home to many wild animals, including bears, wolves, foxes, panthers, otters, porcupines, and more. The park offers a once-in-a-lifetime opportunity to get up close and personal with the animals. There are plenty of fun activities for the whole family.

When visiting Bearizona Wildlife Park, you may expect to see some bears and other wildlife. What you may not expect is the opportunity to do a drive-through of the park. In this park section, you can drive through the open enclosures, seeing the animals in their natural habitat. You will encounter many animals, such as bears walking toward the cars and "wolves stepping into your path to inspect each vehicle" (Kara, 2022).

As you can imagine, there are strict rules when driving through the animal enclosure to keep yourself, your passengers, and the animals safe. You will see the safety rules on signs throughout the drive. They include keeping your windows closed, doors locked, and keeping all parts of your body inside the vehicle at all times. There is also a speed limit while driving to prevent startling or injuring the animals.

After doing a drive-through, you can proceed to the walking area. The Bearizona Wildlife Park has a walk-through area like the ones you will see at zoos. Here, you can see the animals inside their large, open pens. The children can feed the otters, play with the chickens, and admire all the animals in the park. Some permanent park residents include:

- Brown bears
- Black bears
- Panthers
- Porcupines
- Otters
- Chickens
- Foxes
- Wolves
- Elk
- Deer
- Peacocks

A section of the walk-through area includes walking through a tunnel with darkened caves on each side. The caves are animal dens; you can sometimes spot a bear taking an afternoon nap. You may bring your food and drinks into the park, but "there are also snack vendors, a restaurant, and a gift shop for buying treats and souvenirs" (Haveman, 2017).

Rangers and staff at the park are highly informed about all the animals and the park's history. They will share this information as you walk through the park, making it an excellent educational experience for kids. The park is open from 09:00 to 16:00 daily. Weekday park entrance fees are $30 for adults, $20 for children, and $27 for seniors (62+). Weekend fees are $35 for adults, $25 for children, and $32 for seniors.

More Route 66

Route 66 is not only a historical landmark in Williams but also a nod to Williams' past. Route 66 used to be the main route connecting Arizona towns with each other. Route 66 ran through most towns and cities in the state. It was one of the first highways in the United States and opened in 1926. While there are remainders of the route in many towns, the piece remaining in Williams is special.

It was the last section of the entire Route 66 still running. After several legal battles obstructed the completion of Interstate 40 around Williams, it was finally completed in 1984. Part of Route 66 was decommissioned the following year. However, this piece of the road remains relevant and important in Williams to this day. Route 66 is a registered National Historic site with many interesting attractions for locals and tourists alike.

Many people come to Williams to experience this landmark and love taking pictures at the various Route 66 markings along the road. One of the top tourist attractions in Williams is "Pete's Route 66 Gas Station Museum" (Pete's Route 66, n.d.). This gas station is still in its original condition, just as it was when Route 66 was still operational. However, the gas station has now been transformed into a museum, housing artifacts and memorabilia from the era.

Several vintage cars are also displayed at the front of the gas station, making it feel like you have been transported back in time. Pete's Route 66 Gas Station Museum is the perfect place to reflect on the history of Williams and Route 66. It is also the perfect place to take excellent pictures. Furthermore, the gas station has a gift shop where you can buy some interesting souvenirs to remind you of your time in Williams.

Of course, the museum isn't the only note-worthy attraction on Williams' Route 66 section. Some other noteworthy attractions on the Route include:

- Rod's Steakhouse
- Denny's
- Sultana Theater and Bar
- Vaughn's Indian Store
- El Rancho Motel
- Sun Dial Motel

- Hull's Motel Inn
- Mt. Williams Motel
- Red Cross Garage
- Union Station
- Williams Motor Co.

Some diners on Route 66 are still operational and make for the perfect lunch or dinner stop. Be sure to leave enough time for exploring Route 66 when in Williams, as there are many hidden gems on the Route. You can also stay in a restored hotel or motel on the street.

Kaibab National Forest

For an experience in the untamed wild around Williams, head to the Kaibab National Forest. The forest borders the Grand Canyon on both sides, but the Southern Kaibab National Forest is closest to Williams. Kaibab National Forest is open to visitors from all over, and you will have a blast exploring the surroundings.

Many people come to hike and wonder at the beauty of the forest. Several hiking trails are spread throughout the forest—some of the trails take you past the rim of the Grand Canyon. While some trails are more challenging, there are also "13 kid-friendly trails in Kaibab National Forest, including Keyhole Sink Trail, Benham National Recreation Trail, and Sycamore Point Trail" (Best Kid Friendly Trails, n.d.).

You can also go fishing at many of the lakes in the forest. While most rivers only have water during the monsoon season and when the winter snow melts, the rangers and U.S. Forest Services maintain the dams and lakes. You may also kayak on the lakes. However, as these dams supply water to Williams, no swimming is allowed in any lake except White horse lake.

Boating is only allowed on some lakes, including Dogtown and White Horse Lakes, and J.D Dam. You may notice picnic areas and campsites scattered throughout the forest. You are welcome to use these when visiting. No camping is allowed within ¼ mile of water sources to protect wildlife. There aren't any water sources or bathrooms at any of the campsites. Furthermore, there aren't any trash cans at the unmaintained campsites. Remember to take your trash with you.

In addition to the unmaintained campsites in Kaibab National Forest, several developed campsites are also in the forest. These campsites include:

- Kaibab Lake Campground
- Dogtown Lake Campground
- Jakob Lake Campground
- Demotte Campground
- Big Springs Cabin Site

"These campgrounds have picnic tables and fire pits" (Walker, n.d.). Day visitors are also welcome to use these picnic sites, though they may have to pay a fee to do so. Kaibab Lake, Dogtown Lake, and White Horse Lake also have free dumpsites to leave your trash. The campsites are on a first-come, first-serve basis. You can find more information about their prices and availability at the visitor centers.

Kaibab National Forest is the perfect place to bring the family for a fun-filled adventure exploring the wild. There are no fees to enter the park, but most developed camp-sites have a fee. Some areas in the forest also require a permit. An America the Beautiful pass is acceptable in most cases. You can also enquire about the permits at the visitor center when entering the forest.

A Day in Williams

While Williams has so many fantastic experiences to offer, you cannot visit them all in one day. And unfortunately, some people may only have a day to spend in Williams. So, what would you do with a single day in this historic town? Here are a few ideas to get you started.

Visit Pete's Route 66 Gas Station Museum

Can you really say you visited Williams without stopping at Pete's Route 66 Gas Station Museum? I think not. This spot is the perfect place to start your day in Williams, as you get to explore the downtown area, take pictures at the gas station, and see some of the artifacts dating back to the 1900s.

Don't forget to stop by the gift shop for some Route 66 souvenirs and trinkets. I recommend heading to Pete's Gas Station Museum bright and early so you have plenty of time to explore the rest of Route 66 and catch breakfast before heading to your next stop.

Ride the Route 66 Zipline

From Pete's Route 66 Gas Station Museum; your next stop should be at the Route 66 Zipline. The zipline runs

110 feet above the road and gives you a birds-eye view of Route 66 and Williams. The zipline has a top speed of 30 mph.

While it isn't scary, it is a thrilling experience. The zipline takes you across Route 66 multiple times, giving you plenty of time to enjoy the view and spot some locations you want to visit next. "The Route 66 zipline is priced at $12 per person" (Family-Fun Weekend, n.d.). There is a height requirement for the zipline, so small children may not be able to enjoy this adventure.

Ride the Grand Canyon Railway

The best way to experience the Grand Canyon is by train. While the Grand Canyon Railway is a more expensive outing, it is filled with fun, relaxation, and beautiful views. Arrive in time to see the Western shootout, experience the thrill of robbers on the train, and see the Grand Canyon in style.

The Grand Canyon Railway is fun for the whole family. You don't have to worry about driving on the highway to the Grand Canyon. Instead, sit back and enjoy the view and live music on the train.

Go to Bearizona

Bearizona is one activity you cannot skip out on when visiting Williams. It's not every day you get to see so many wild animals in such a short time. It's also not every day you can drive in an open enclosure surrounded by bears, wolves, and other animals.

This is the perfect way to spend an afternoon in Williams. Your kids will love it, and so will you. If you enjoy learning about the wild animals of North America, this is the perfect stop.

As you can see, Williams is a small town with a giant heart. The town does an excellent job of entertaining thousands of tourists annually. With so many wonderful things to see and do, it's no surprise that everyone who visits Arizona wants to make the trip to Williams.

If you are looking for a spookier time in Arizona, fear not. The following town has many ghost stories and a moving history sure to keep even the greatest thrill-seekers satisfied.

3

JEROME

My idea of heaven is being in Arizona, stuck up a mountain-somewhere where there are no phones. –Gavin Esler

This quote comes to mind when I think of Jerome. Because the town is built against a hill, it feels like you are on a mountain when visiting, and the views of the Verde Valley are amazing from Jerome. Jerome is a short drive Southeast of Flagstaff with many similarities with the abovementioned city.

While Jerome is now a town known for its sliding buildings, ghost stories, and artists, it plays an important part in the history of Arizona. Like many other cities in this state, Jerome's story begins with a mine.

A Little Bit of History

The earliest records of people inhabiting the area of Jerome and the Verde Valley are from the 1100s. Like Flagstaff, the area was inhabited by Sinagua tribes and other Native American clans. By the 1500s, they had left the area for no apparent reason. At this time, the Yavapai people resided in the area. They used copper pigments in the mountains around them to dye their faces and clothes.

They were left in relative peace during the Spanish Inquisition in the 1500s because the Spanish saw little use for copper. Instead, they were searching for gold. However, in the 1850s, when Arizona became a part of North America, the Yavapai people were relocated to the Verde Valley reservation and later to the San Carlos reservation.

When the copper mines were discovered in the area, plenty of people flooded here to start mining. Jerome was named after Eugene Jerome, one of the wealthy financiers of the United Verde Copper Company, who bought the mining rights in the Verde Valley.

In 1883, Jerome opened a post office and was officially recognized as a town (Weiser, 2022). By 1900, Jerome had expanded so much that the Montana Hotel, with 200 rooms, was opened to accommodate the miners and visitors. Jerome continued to grow and develop. The owner of the mines, William Clark, ensured that they used the newest technology at the copper mines in and around Jerome. In 1909, Jerome even had a small locomotive railway that connected with the main lines to transport the copper mined around town.

Jerome was incorporated in 1899 because of the town's need for order and safety standards. By this time, Jerome was known as "the wickedest town of the West" (Young, n.d.) because of all the saloons and brothels present. The lack of safety standards also led to frequent fires ravaging the town.

In the following years, Jerome saw times of prosperity and hardship. In the 1930s, during the great depression, Jerome was nearly crippled into extinction. Phelps Dodge bought the mining rights in 1935 and continued to mine copper in the area until the closing of the mines in 1952.

At that time, only about 100 residents lived in Jerome, and the town was considered a ghost town. That changed in the 1960s when newcomers moved to Jerome to experience the old West. They established an artistic community in the old town and lived among the fallen buildings.

Today, Jerome is known as an artist district with around 400 permanent residents. Most tourists come to Jerome to witness the fallen buildings and ruins of the mines and to catch a glimpse of what the wild west was once like.

And if you are interested in visiting the area, you might also be interested to know what draws people to Jerome specifically. There are several activities and attractions that make people stop at Jerome when in Arizona.

Jerome State Historic Park

One of the first stops you should make in any town, especially one like Jerome, is at the museum. And the Jerome Museum is located in the Douglas Mansion in what is now known as Jerome State Historic Park. While the mansion was remodeled to serve as the museum in the 1960s, it was once the private residence of the Douglas family. James Douglas built the mansion in 1916 on the hill above his mine, Little Daisy ("Facility Information," n.d.).

The mansion was initially used as the Douglas family's private home and as a hotel for investors at the mine. The descendants of James Douglas later sold the mansion and estate to the state, and the Jerome State Historic Park was officially opened in 1965.

You can visit the state park and Douglas mansion in Jerome. The state park now has a picnic area and beautiful scenery as it overlooks the Verde Valley below. Some rooms, including one bathroom and the library in the mansion, were restored to their original layout, giving you a sense of what the mansion would have looked like in the 1920s. You can tour the mansion, where the history of the Douglas family and Jerome is on display.

Outside, you will also see some mining artifacts and an original Ford Model 1 car that used to belong to someone in Jerome. The museum also houses many mining artifacts, including pieces of ore found in the mines. Of course, scientific exhibits also explain how the mining industry in Jerome operated.

You can have a picnic outside where the children can

explore the state grounds. Jerome State Historic Park is another park where children between six and twelve may earn their junior ranger badges. You can find more information about the junior ranger program at the visitor center.

If you want to visit Jerome State Historic Park, you must pay the entry fees at the front office. The fees for adults are $7 per person, while children between seven and thirteen pay $4. Children under six may enter the park for free.

The Sliding Jail

One of the most interesting things about Jerome is how evident the environmental effects of the mining operations are on the town. When mining for gold, silver, or copper, the miners used dynamite explosives to blow holes into the mountain. These activities leave the ground unstable and make ground shifts more common.

Pair that with the mountainside on which Jerome was built and the fault lines underneath the town, and you have a recipe for disaster. Since its origins, buildings in Jerome have been known to shift and slide downhill. And while many buildings have been lost forever, one remains and is clear evidence of the shifting ground beneath Jerome.

The sliding jail is the most prominent example of how much ground shifting has occurred in Jerome due to mining expeditions. The jail started sliding downhill in

1935 and has since moved more than 200 feet from its original location. The state acquired the rights to the jail in
2017, and it has since been stabilized to keep it from
moving or crumbling. Many people come to Jerome to see
the sliding jail, as it is one of a few buildings that show how
the ground beneath the town has shifted. The concrete jail
cell was part of a larger building made of wood and tin.
However, this is the only part that remained intact.

You can visit the sliding jail for free, and it is difficult
to miss as it is obviously out of place. Other buildings also
show evidence of the shifting ground beneath Jerome,
including the Cuban Queen, of which the front face of the
building crumbled in 2017. Many of the historical buildings in Jerome have undergone safety tests. They have
been made secure to prevent them from caving in or sliding, too.

However, this was not always the case. There are likely
many other buildings that once stood in Jerome, which
you can no longer see today because they have slid down
the mountain.

Jerome Ghost Tours

Many people believe that Jerome is haunted. While
people still live in the town, many consider it a ghost
town. This is partly because of how many abandoned
buildings are in town and partly because of the controver-
sial history of Jerome. The many fires, mining incidents,
and saloon brawls led to several deaths in Jerome's history,

and some believe that the ghosts of the deceased still walk around town.

As such, there are several ghost tours in and around Jerome. Most tours take you to similar places, including the Haskins House, the sliding jail, the Crib's section and its female prison, and many more. Most tours are limited to 12 or 14 guests and require that you book in advance. There are also some private tours available. Some of the Best Jerome ghost tours include:

- Pandora's Box Ghost Adventure: $84 per person
- Jerome Haunted Tour: $45 per person ($20 for children between 7 and 12)
- Jerome Ghost Adventure: $70 per person
- Jerome Ghost Walk: $45 per person

While most of these tours don't have a specific age restriction, some ask that you leave children younger than seven at home for this one. Not only is the theme unsuitable for young children, but most tours require a lot of walking, which may be problematic for children.

Suppose you are a true thrill seeker and aren't entirely satisfied with a two-hour ghost tour. In that case, you can also stay in "the most haunted place in Arizona" (Topor, 2021), The Jerome Grand Hotel. So, what makes this hotel the most haunted place?

Likely the fact that the hotel used to be the United Verde Hospital. Many people who worked at the mines or lived in town died at this hospital. In addition, the natural disasters and accidents, including fires and floods, caused many souls to perish in Jerome. The hospital was initially built in 1917 and rebuilt in 1926 after mining explosions destroyed it.

In 1950, the hospital was abandoned after Jerome was all but a ghost town. The equipment inside was left untouched for nearly 20 years, after which the state removed it due to safety concerns. The caretaker of the building committed suicide after 20 years of watching over it, which points to the ominous mood surrounding the site.

The hospital was turned into the Jerome Grand Hotel in 1994 and officially opened in 1996. You can now book your stay at the hotel but do so at your own risk. The hotel's interior is modeled after the 1930s, and many of the artifacts and art in the hotel are initially from that period in Jerome.

You can also eat dinner at the Asylum, the hotel's restaurant. Here, the drinks are creatively named after some of the medicines and medicinal practices of the time. There is also a gift shop in what used to be the hospital's emergency room. Many guests at the hotel report strange experiences, including hearing and smelling things that aren't there.

So, if you are in the mood for ghost hunting, Jerome is one place in Arizona you shouldn't miss.

Gold King Mine and Ghost Town

If you still have some time left in Jerome, I would recommend taking a walk up to the Gold King Mine and ghost town. This area was once a town/suburb known as Haynes. It even had a post office for a short while. Haynes was also a mining town. However, while Jerome was known for its copper mines, Haynes was a gold mine.

After the vein dried up in 1914, the town only had about 14 residents, who also cleared out soon after. In 1960, the mine was converted into the tourist attraction it is now. Hundreds of vintage cars, trucks, and vehicles are parked at the mine. You can take a stroll through the old village, where you will see some of the original buildings, like a sawmill and blacksmith.

Other buildings, including a schoolhouse, dentist, and shoe repair shop, were also brought in. For those brave enough, you can also go down into the original gold mine shaft while touring the area. Furthermore, you can see plenty of mining artifacts and equipment. Some of them are still in working condition.

There is a petting zoo for children, and you can also arrange to pan for gold at the site. While there is still some gold to be found, you must call ahead and ask if the weather permits gold panning when you plan to go. The Gold King mine and ghost town is a perfect family stop, and given its proximity to Jerome, you can visit the mine on the same day.

Ticket prices for entering the site are $12 for people between 13 and 79. People older than 80 and children younger than six can visit the Gold King mine free of charge. Children between six and 12 pay $7. If you want to pan for gold, you will also pay $18 per person, and panning for other gems is priced at $12 per person.

A Day in Jerome

Suppose you only have one day to spend in Jerome. In that case, you may wonder what the best activities are. Unfortunately, you won't have time to fit everything mentioned above into a single day. Still, you would be surprised to learn how much you could get done. Here is an example of a great one-day itinerary for Jerome.

Take a 1-Hour Tour

There are many ghost tours available in Jerome. And the great news is that most of them are only about an hour long. So, you could easily fit one of these tours into your schedule. The tours take you to many exciting destinations in Jerome, allowing you to see more of the town than you would have if you had not taken the tour. Some excellent one-hour tours include:

- The Spirit Walk Tour
- Get the History Shuttle Tour
- Jerome Haunted History Shuttle
- The Original Jerome Ghost Adventure

Most of these tours require advance booking, and some have age restrictions due to the nature of the tour.

Visit Jerome State Historic Park

If you are keen to learn about the history of Jerome and some of the prominent families who shaped the town, then a visit to Jerome State Historic Park is highly recommended. Here, you will have pristine views of the Verde Valley and learn more about the Douglas family and their role in Jerome's past.

You can also enjoy lunch at one of the picnic tables in the park. While visiting, the children can explore the area and earn their junior ranger badges.

Eat Lunch at the Haunted Hamburger

If you plan to go out for lunch, one restaurant stands out from the crowd. The Haunted Hamburger is a casual dining restaurant that offers delicious food at an affordable price. This is the perfect restaurant to bring the family.

However, if you are looking for somewhere more unique to eat lunch or dinner, you can also try out the Asylum, the restaurant at the Jerome Grand Hotel. Although the Asylum's prices are steeper, it is a once-in-a-lifetime opportunity to eat a meal in an abandoned, remodeled, and haunted hospital.

See the Sliding Jail

If your short, guided tour of Jerome doesn't include a stop at the sliding jail, you must take the time to visit this site. The sliding jail is one of the main tourist attractions in Jerome, and it has an interesting history explained at the site. The sliding jail is literally a jail cell that has slid more than 200 feet from its original location due to ground shifts from mining explosions. It is a testament to the destruction of the explosive used to mine copper.

Stop by the Mine Museum

Finally, before you depart from Jerome, you should make a pit stop at the Mine Museum. The Mine Museum shares information about the mining history of Jerome. It also shows how many people from different cultures came to Jerome to be a part of the mining industry.

Mining and gambling artifacts, daily household items, and objects from the hospital are on display at the museum. You can learn what life was like for the miners, the brothel keepers, and the civilians who lived in Jerome at the time. You can also learn more about the prominent families who funded the mining operations and established Jerome as a town.

Jerome might not be a developing city like many other destinations in Arizona. Still, it is a town where you can experience what life was like at the beginning of the 20th century in Arizona. Jerome is the perfect place if you enjoy ghost stories, history, and art. If not, don't worry. Plenty of other destinations worth visiting in Arizona are sure to tickle your interest.

4

PAGE

Arizona-land of extremes. Land of contrasts. Land of surprises.
Land of contradictions. –n.d.

Who would have thought that one of the most spectacular water features would appear right in the heart of the desert? I'm talking of Lake Powell, which is just one of the amazing things to experience when visiting the town of Page.

What's interesting about this spot is that it wasn't founded because of mining activities. Many other cities and towns in Arizona were originally mining or lumber towns. However, Page's origins are quite different. While this town now has about 8,000 permanent residents, it sees nearly three million tourists annually. Why is that, you might ask?

Before you learn about what you can do and see in Page, it is a great idea to learn more about its origins first. So, let's start by explaining a little bit of Page's history.

A Little Bit of History

Page is one of the newest towns in Arizona and the entire United States. It was officially opened as a town on the first of March, 1975. And 30 years prior, there hadn't been a single building in the area, at least not a Western-style one. Before the arrival of the construction workers, the area where Page is now located belonged to the Navajo tribes.

When Arizona became a part of the United States, Page saw one of the biggest construction projects of the time. That was the project of building the Glen Canyon Dam, and it started in 1956. The dam was built to provide water to the Southwestern states of the USA.

When the first contractors arrived, Page was nothing more than a few dirt roads and trailer homes. The government camp, as it was first called, was built atop the Manson Mesa peak and overlooked the canyon below. In the seven years it took to construct the dam, permanent homes were steadily built in the area, followed by several churches, a post office, and other buildings. A total of 12 churches received ground in Page, and the area where they stand is still known as "church row" (City of Page, n.d.).

When the dam was completed in 1963, many residents had moved away again. The permanent houses built in Page remained and were sold for a very reasonable price.

Most of the remaining people were workers at the dam or surrounding areas. Page was officially recognized as a town in 1975, making it one of the youngest towns in America.

Most people living in Page today still work at the Glen Canyon Dam, overseeing the water storage and hydroelectric plant facilities. Despite the town still being minute compared to other cities, Page sees more than three million tourists annually. Why do all these people come to Page, one might ask?

Well, there are several reasons for visiting Page. Whether you are interested in exploring the natural scenery or want to witness one of the most impressive dams in the country, Page has something for everyone.

Antelope Canyon

If you enjoy hiking trails and seeing beautiful scenery, Antelope Canyon should be on your bucket list. This slot canyon was formed by thousands of years of soil erosion. As a result, the water running through the canyon has left some of the most unique shapes and swirls on the canyon walls. And, because the canyon is mostly closed at the top, the light beams that shine through make this canyon a magical place for hikers and photographers alike.

Antelope Canyon has two hiking sections: Upper Antelope and Lower Antelope. Both offer stunning views, but the Upper Antelope trail is more popular among tourists because it isn't such a steep hike. It is more child friendly, and the trail is generally easier to complete.

Lower Antelope Canyon requires climbing many stairs and ladders into the canyon. There are several uneven sections, making this a more difficult hike. While the upper Antelope is an A-shaped canyon (it is broadest at the bottom), the lower Antelope is a V-shaped canyon (narrowest at the bottom). This also means that the way the light reflects in the canyon differs depending on which section you hike (Cole, 2022).

You can only visit Antelope Canyon with an authorized Navajo guide. There are a couple of reasons why this is the case:

- First, Antelope Canyon is part of the Navajo reservation, and you require special permission to come onto the reservation and access the canyon.
- Antelope Canyon is a sacred place for the Navajo people. You must respect it and shouldn't damage or vandalize the canyon in any way.
- Finally, because flash floods sometimes occur in the canyon and can become lethal without warning, you need a professional guide who knows what to look for when hiking the trail.

These factors mean that you must pre-book your trip to Antelope Canyon. There are different tours, depending on if you are going on the trail as a photographer or a casual hiker. Because of the narrow canyon walls, you may only bring a small bag for water, sunscreen, or other essentials on the hike.

No tripods, selfie sticks, or large bags are allowed on the trail. You are also not permitted to bring food into the canyon. Remember to pack up everything you bring with you. There aren't any trashcans or bathrooms once you leave the visitor center at the start of the trail.

You don't require any special equipment to hike Antelope Canyon. But it is recommended that you wear stable, closed-toe shoes and layered clothing as temperatures often change in the canyon. Also, wear a hat and sunscreen. Bring a bandana, handkerchief, or glasses to shield your eyes and face against the sand. A small water bottle is permitted and recommended on the hike.

Antelope Canyon is an easy enough trail to hike for children, especially the upper part of the trail. To reach the upper section of Antelope Canyon, however, you must drive on the back of a truck from the visitor center. If your children still use car seats, you must provide your own for the drive. You cannot bring strollers or baby carriers into the canyon.

Because you need a tour guide for Antelope Canyon, some costs are involved. The price for the trail depends on which section of the trail you are hiking and whether you are going as a hiker or photographer. There are only limited slots available for photographers as they take up a lot of time.

A one-hour hike generally costs between $40 and $80, while a 90-minute hike is generally priced between $50 and $90. The price might be slightly less for children.

This fee usually includes the park permit of $8, but that depends on the tour you have booked.

Powell Museum

If you are interested in learning more about Page's history and why it was chosen as the location for the Glen Canyon Dam, then a trip to the Powell Museum is in order. The museum is located in what was once a concrete lab for testing the dam's strength before and during its construction.

Today, you can learn about the history of Page, Lage Powell, the dam, and the Navajo people who inhabited the area before it became a building site. In addition, you can find many interesting artifacts and exhibitions at the museum. There are also monthly lectures about the history of Page and the surrounding area, which are free to attend.

Although there aren't any special activities for children at Powell Museum, they are welcome to visit. Many exhibitions have interactive sections; children will enjoy learning about Page's history. The museum also has a gift shop where you can buy Page-themed souvenirs to remind you of your time there.

The Powell Museum, like Lake Powell, is named in honor of Major John Wesley Powell. He was a war veteran and explorer. He led one of the first expeditions of the Colorado River and is responsible for mapping much of the area. Although Powell died long before the dam's construction and founding of Page began, the lake and museum are named in his honor.

You will also see many of Powell's sketches and journal entries of the area. In addition to the exhibits, you can also watch videos about the construction of the dam and Lake Powell.

Entrance to the museum is priced at $7 per adult (13-59). Children aged five to 12 pay $2, while seniors and military personnel pay $6 for entry. There is also a special family package available for $15.

Glen Canyon Dam

Of course, one of the main attractions in Page is the Glen Canyon Dam. Considering the town only exists today because of its construction, it should be no surprise that many people travel to this town situated on Manson Mesa, especially to witness this marvel. I recommend visiting the museum first to learn more about the history and construction of the dam. Doing so will help you appreciate the dam all the more.

Glen Canyon Dam is the second tallest concrete-arch dam, with a height of 710 feet. The dam is a water storage for most cities in Arizona and surrounding states. Furthermore, it made the construction of the Glen Canyon Hydropower station possible. This hydroelectric power station helps supply many cities in Western North America with power.

There are plenty of fun things to do when visiting Glen Canyon Dam, but the best place to start is the Carl

Hayden Visitor Center. You can walk around this small but informative visitor center to learn more about the dam's construction, importance, and maintenance.

There are also dam tours you can take, which you can pre-book or book at the visitor center. The tours cost $15 per family. The tour guide starts his tour by taking you around the visitor center and explaining some of the details of the Glen Canyon Dam and its importance. Then, you go outside and take a walk along the dam.

You even get the opportunity to go down to the dam's base, where you can walk around on the neatly mowed lawn that helps cushion the dam. Once finished, you may also walk on the Glen Canyon bridge, which has a spectacular view over the dam and surrounding area.

The tour is very informative and entertaining, making it suitable for the whole family. The visitor center is also packed with interactive exhibitions for children. Furthermore, children between six and twelve can earn their junior ranger badges. You can find more information on this project at the front desk or online.

Entering the visitor center is free of charge. The only fees you have to pay are the tour fees if you want to take the group tour. Tour prices are as follows:

- Family groups: $15
- Adults: $5
- Seniors (65+): $4
- Children (7-16): $2.50

Lake Powell

While most people who visit Page go to the Glen Canyon Museum and explore the other attractions too, other people who come here are primarily here to experience Lake Powell. Although it is named a lake, Lake Powell is actually an artificial reservoir that resulted from the construction of the Glen Canyon Dam.

Like the museum, Lake Powell is named after John Wesley Powell, without whose discoveries, there probably wouldn't even be a lake. Lake Powell was recognized as part of the Glen Canyon National Recreation Area in 1972, which is still a part today ("Page Lake Powell Information," n.d.).

And even though Lake Powell is artificial and not even an actual lake, many people—as many as 3 million per year-come to Page to do lake activities at Lake Powell. Some of these activities include:

- Hiking trips
- Skiing
- Staying on a houseboat
- Kayaking
- Fishing
- Having a "beach day"
- Camping

There are various tours to take around Lake Powell, and many people bring their boats for a summer holiday at the lake. Lake Powell is also a popular spring break destination. Many people come to Lake Powell to enjoy a summer holiday in the middle of the desert. The beautiful scenery and interesting landscape make Lake Powell a one-of-a-kind destination.

There are many camping spots, hotels, resorts, and family units along Lake Powell where you can reside while enjoying the lake during the day. At night, there are also many restaurants to try out. Regardless of your life-style, you will surely have fun at Lake Powell.

Of course, there are many fun things for kids to do too. They can play in the sand and water, learn to kayak, fish, and take a boat trip. Parental supervision is recommended at the beachfront, especially during the busier seasons.

Visiting Lake Powell is free. However, you will need to book accommodation and tours at additional costs. Some camping spots also require a permit. The price of these activities depends on which company you use and how long you plan to stay.

Lake Powell is an excellent spot to do it regardless of what you enjoy doing. Staying at the lake ensures you have a beautiful view and are close to many other attractions in and around Page.

Horseshoe Bend

The Horseshoe Bend is equally as popular as Lake Powell and sees nearly three million tourists every year. While Lake Powell is an artificial attraction, nothing about the Horseshoe Bend is artificial. This 270° bend in the

Colorado river (Huddlebee, 2022) was formed along with the rest of the canyon over millions of years.

There is a lookout point where you can see the entire Horseshoe Bend from high above the river. You can also take a helicopter ride to see it from even higher or go for a kayaking tour and experience the Horseshoe Bend from below.

You must make a short 1.5-mile roundtrip hike to reach the lookout point. While this is an easy hike, closed, sturdy shoes are recommended. Also, bring enough water, sunscreen, and a hat, as there aren't shaded areas along the trail or at the lookout. There aren't any bathrooms on the trail, so you should visit the one at the trail-head/parking before starting the hike.

Remember to pack everything you brought on the trail, and don't make carvings on the sandstone walls or leave litter behind. There are guardrails at the lookout, but it is still recommended that you watch your footing and keep track of young children.

The hike is easy enough to do with children, as there isn't an incline either way, and the path is broad. However, the path isn't paved, making it unsuitable for strollers. It might also be a challenging hike for those who fear heights, as the lookout point isn't fenced around, and the height is quite daunting. Keep away from the edge of the lookout to prevent accidents.

Getting to the Horseshoe Bend lookout is easy enough without a professional tour guide. However, I recommend going early in the day to avoid the crowds and the Arizonian heat. The parking lot at the trailhead fills up quickly, and the lookout is often very crowded. You will need to pay for the parking at the trailhead, which is $10 per car.

Grand Staircase-Escalante National Monument

If you are looking for a bit more of a challenge than the short hikes around Page, like Antelope Canyon and the trail to the Horseshoe Bend, you should try hiking into the Grand Staircase-Escalante National Monument. The Grand Staircase-Escalante National Monument is a vast area—1.88 million acres to be exact (Rose, 2019) of protected land. The Monument stretched from Utah into Arizona and beyond.

Several hiking trails in the Grand Staircase-Escalante National Monument vary in difficulty and length. Most people on the trail camp at one of the many camping sites. And although there aren't fees payable to hike into the monument, the camping sites charge per night you spend there.

The Grand Staircase-Escalante National Monument is surrounded by multiple visitor centers. These centers allow you to learn more about the history of the monument, and some even have a junior ranger program for children. The Grand Staircase-Escalante National Monument has quite a fascinating history.

The Pueblo tribes (Native American tribes) once called this area home. They were farmers and hunter-gatherers who flourished in such a harsh and unforgiving environment. You can see rock paintings and ruins of granaries and campsites at various points in the monument.

The Grand Staircase-Escalante is also a crucial historical site that has given scientists a lot of data about the time of the dinosaurs and how they became extinct. As such, the entire monument site is extremely valuable for scientists of many areas and environmentalists.

It is, therefore, critical that you protect the area wherever possible. This means following the "pack it in, pack it out" rules of hiking. Leave the park as undisturbed as possible to preserve it for coming generations.

Speaking of coming generations, there are several kid-friendly hikes in the Grand Staircase-Escalante National Monument, including Lick Wash Slot Canyon and Willis Creek Slot Canyon. A hiking trip to the monument is the perfect way to teach children about the environment and the importance of protecting it.

Although the Grand Staircase-Escalante is not an attraction confined to Page, it is one of many interesting places to visit while there.

Vermillion Cliffs National Monument

Vermillion Cliffs National Monument is another protected area near Page. This monument has as many impressive attractions as the Grand Staircase-Escalante National Monument, including one in particular: The Wave. The wave is a magnificent rock formation that formed due to water erosion over millions of years.

To reach the wave, you will need a special permit to

access the Wire Pass trailhead, located in the North Coyote Buttes Wilderness area, which is a part of the Vermillion Cliffs National Monument. Unfortunately, obtaining this permit is no easy feat. Only 12 to 64 permits are extended daily via lottery. You have to apply for the permit online well in advance.

Therefore, I recommend applying when you have a planned date for visiting Page. If you are lucky enough to get a North Coyote Buttes pass, you can get to the Wave with an off-road vehicle. Most roads in the Vermillion Cliffs National Monument area are in poor condition, so a capable off-road vehicle is required.

If you cannot visit the Wave, there are still plenty of other hiking trails, camping spots, and off-roading excursions to enjoy. The hiking trails differ in length and difficulty. And, while some trails might be easy enough for children, it's essential to know about the risks of hiking in Vermillion Cliffs National Monument.

Because the area is so vast and remote, getting help in an emergency is difficult. There are many poisonous animals in the monument. Flash floods and extreme temperatures are also common in the area. So, suppose you decide to go on a hike in Vermillion Cliffs National Park. In that case, arriving well-prepared for any disaster is important. Young children cannot keep up on some hiking trails, and I don't recommend bringing someone with mobility problems or health issues on a hike in the monument.

Suppose you want to experience the Vermillion Cliffs National Monument but don't want to stay inside it. In that case, I recommend staying at one of the campsites bordering the monument. Stateline Campgrounds and Whitehouse Campsite are developed camping spots perfect for enjoying the secludedness of the monument.

Neither campsites require permits nor camping fees. And, although they aren't on monument property, they border it. This means you will still experience the spectacular views and atmosphere of the Vermillion Cliffs National Monument without facing as many risks.

A Day in Page

One day in Page is hardly enough time to experience everything the area offers. But you can still get a sense of what the town and surrounding area offer in a single day if you plan the day correctly. Planning is essential when you only have a limited time in a town like Page.

So, what should you do with your 24 hours in this town? Look at this excellent itinerary example for inspiration on what to do with a day in Page.

Go to Antelope Canyon

A trip to Antelope Canyon will only take two hours and is the perfect way to start your day in Page. Remember to book in advance. If you are strapped for time, I recommend doing this hike first thing. It won't be as hot, and it gives you the rest of the day to explore other areas. You can do the Antelope Upper or Lower hike. Or you can attempt both if you have enough time.

Try Big John's Texas BBQ.

After the draining Antelope Canyon hike, you will no

doubt need some food. And, according to anyone who has visited Page, myself included, there is one place you cannot pass by. Big John's Texas BBQ delivers delicious BBQ food at a reasonable price.

This restaurant is the perfect place to enjoy a delicious burger or rack of ribs with a cold beer. It is located at Lake Powell, giving you an excellent view to complete your meal. After enjoying a great lunch, you can walk around the lake, go swimming, or enjoy some ice cream at one of the other restaurants or shops in the area.

Visit the Glen Canyon Dam

After lunch, you can visit the Glen Canyon Dam. A trip to Page isn't complete without seeing the reason why the town exists at all. If you have two hours to spare, I strongly urge you to take the tour at the dam's visitor center. It will give you much more information about the dam, making your experience more authentic. It is also the perfect way to entertain the family.

Don't forget to stop by the visitor center, where the kids can explore. You can also learn more about the Glen Canyon Dam, Lake Powell, and Page's history at the visitor center. Of course, you can also buy some souvenirs.

Watch the Sunset at Horseshoe Bend

Finally, you cannot leave Page without seeing Horseshoe Bend. Although the view from the lookout point is spectacular at any time of day, it is a unique experience to stare out over the Colorado River at sunset. The sunlight causes the red sandstone to light up in the most amazing colors, making the entire bend look like a glowing ember.

The short trek to the lookout point is also the perfect way to work off the delicious meal you had for lunch.

Page is a town with a fascinating history and plenty of worthwhile attractions. It is the perfect place for photographers—amateur or professional—and guarantees an authentic Arizonan experience.

But if you aren't heading toward Page while in Arizona, fear not. There are still several other towns and cities worth visiting, like Phoenix, which is the next stop in this guide.

5

PHOENIX

Arizona is known for five 'Cs'—copper, citrus, cotton, cattle, and climate. –Kathleen Derzipilski

P hoenix is likely one of the most famous cities in Arizona. In 2021, a recorded 1.6 million people permanently resided in Phoenix. And although it is now the biggest city in the state, it has a humble origin story. Before we consider what fun things you can keep busy with in Phoenix, let's first recount the history of this state's capital city.

A Little Bit of History

Phoenix's history can be traced back thousands of years to when the Hohokam people inhabited the area. Despite the dry and unforgiving environment, the Hohokam tribes made a living here by farming animals and grains like corn and legumes. Evidence shows they also "also carried out extensive trade with nearby Anasazi, Mogollon, and other Mesoamerican tribes" ("Phoenix-mythology," n.d.).

The Hohokam people were extremely innovative and dug miles of irrigation canals in the earth on what is now Phoenix to deliver water to the valley. This made the soil fertile and allowed them to grow crops in an otherwise bone-dry area. Scientists suspect that the Hohokam people abandoned the area between 1350 and 1400 due to extreme droughts and flash floods.

Many, many years later, the area where Phoenix is now located was discovered by Jack Swillings, a prominent war veteran. He came across the area while looking for a place to make a fortune in the 1850s. When he noticed the wide, open expanses, he realized that this would make for perfect farmlands, as there was no frost or snow in winter. The valley was also perfect for farming because of how wide and flat it was. The only thing missing was water.

So, Swillings founded the Swillings Irrigation Canal Company, moved to the site, and began digging irrigation trenches in 1867. He used the grid line left there by the Hohokam people to guide his canals. One year later, water from the Salt River flowed into the canal, and more people moved to the area to farm the land.

The town was then named Phoenix after several debates among the inhabitants. Eventually, they settled on Phoenix because, just like the bird, Phoenix's civilization would rise from the ashes of its previous inhabitants. The post office was erected in 1868 when Phoenix was officially declared a town. It was incorporated in 1881. By this time, Phoenix had several churches, a hospital, a school, and a population of 2500 residents.

Unlike many other cities and towns in Arizona, Phoenix did not make a name because of mining. And as such, the town did not fall into ruin when the mines dried up. Instead, people moved to the area to farm newly bought land. They expanded their farmlands, and that is how Phoenix grew.

Today, Phoenix is a bustling city. Many people still farm in the surrounding areas, and several irrigation systems, all thanks to those created by the Hohokam people, ensure a stable water supply to the area. The backbone of Phoenix's economy rests on copper, climate, cattle, citrus, and cotton. These sectors have driven Phoenix for centuries and will likely continue to do so for many centuries more.

As someone traveling through Phoenix, you may wonder what makes Phoenix an attractive tourist destination. Well, as you will soon see, Phoenix has many exciting sites and activities, some of which you will undoubtedly want to visit when passing through the city.

Arizona Capitol Museum

Your first stop in Phoenix should be at the Arizona Capitol Museum. The Arizona Capitol Museum is located in downtown Phoenix, in what used to be the Capitol building when Phoenix became the state capital in 1901. The building was repurposed as a museum which opened in 1977 (Williams, 2022). Despite having undergone some changes during the past 100 years, the Arizona Capitol Museum Building was kept as close to the original building as possible.

This means you shouldn't expect fancy artifacts or high-tech rooms when visiting. Instead, you will experience what the building looked like when it was first built. The museum shares information about the history of Phoenix and the state of Arizona. You can learn about the Native Americans who first called the area home, the influential people who made Arizona what it is today and the development of the state over the years.

There is a gift shop in the Museum where you can buy history books about Phoenix and Arizona. You can also buy trinkets and souvenirs to remind you of your trip to Arizona's capital city. Lectures and presentations are frequently held at the museum, where you can learn more about the Phoenix's history from some of the experts.

You can take a tour through the museum hosted by one of the museum tour guides. You may be interested in looking at many interesting artifacts and models in the museum. Although the museum doesn't have an area dedicated to children, the staff are friendly and accommodating to their needs. Older children may have fun learning about Phoenix, and they will enjoy some of the artifacts.

A tour through the museum usually takes about 45 minutes to one hour. If your children are too young to stay patient throughout the tour, leaving them at home for this activity might be best. Fortunately, entrance to the museum and guest lectures are always free, so you can bring your children anytime.

I recommend consulting the Arizona Capitol Museum website before a visit to see if any special events, like lectures or presentations, are happening. This will help you plan your trip better. It will also help you familiarize yourself with the museum, so you know exactly what to expect when you arrive. The Arizona Capitol Museum is sure to be an insightful experience and should therefore be one of your first stops in the city.

Arizona Science Center

If a museum isn't your thing, you might be interested in visiting a science museum instead. The Arizona Science Center is also located in downtown Phoenix and is within walking distance from the Capital Museum. However, when walking in downtown Phoenix, especially between the Capital Museum and Science Center, avoid the home-less tent city between the buildings. There have been incidents of theft and violence.

The Arizona Science Center offers a whole other experience than a normal museum. Architect Antoine Predock constructed the building, and the building itself is a testament to what lies inside. The Arizona Science Center has many exciting interactive exhibits, a huge movie theater, and a planetarium. You can learn about the most recent scientific discoveries. You can also play with the interactive exhibits found throughout the center. New exhibits are frequently added, so you don't have to worry about boredom when you return.

The Arizona Science Center is meant to be a hands-on experience. Therefore, children of all ages and adults are guaranteed an excellent time when visiting. Guides explain how the exhibits work and are there to answer any questions you may have. In addition to visiting the science center, you can also visit the five-story screen theater to watch movies and series about the scientific exhibits in the center. Furthermore, you can visit the planetarium to learn more about the stars and the universe.

All exhibits at the science center cater to children and adults. So, you won't have any problems keeping the younger ones entertained while the older children have fun. The Science Center is meant to be an excursion for the whole family.

Of course, there are some entrance fees to consider when visiting the Arizona Science Center. The general entry fee is as follows:

- Adults: $22
- Children (3-17): $16
- Seniors (65+): $20

Visiting the screen theater and planetarium comes at an additional cost. These add-ons cost $9 for adults and seniors and $8 for children (7-13).

Camelback Mountain

Camelback Mountain is one of the top tourist attractions in Phoenix. The mountain is visible in the skyline from anywhere in Phoenix. And although it is a short, 2.5-mile out-and-back trail, it is rated as a difficult to extremely difficult hike. You can follow two trails up Camelback Mountain: Echo Canyon Trail and Cholla Trail. Both trails are the same length, and they are also equally difficult.

However, despite their difficulty, most hikers have no regrets after completing this grueling hike. They agree that "the 360-degree views from the summit are worth it" ("Camelback Mountain," n.d.). From the Camelback Mountain peak, you can see all the way over Phoenix and the surrounding area.

There are some steep sections on the hike, and some sections on the trail require hand-over-hand climbing. Therefore, you should bring a bladder for water instead of walking with a bottle in your hands. Because of the trail's difficulty, I don't think it is wise to bring children. Children younger than three definitely won't be able to do the hike, and children younger than 10 likely won't finish it. You cannot safely bring a stroller or carry a baby in a kangaroo pouch on this trail.

The trail requires a reasonable level of fitness and mobility to complete, which is why you should assess your fitness level before attempting it. In addition, there are some things you should keep in mind that will make it easier to complete this trail:

- Start hiking early in the morning or later in the afternoon to avoid the midday heat.
- Wear sturdy shoes that protect your feet and ankles.
- Wear a hat, sunscreen, and sunglasses.
- Bring a water bladder instead of a bottle.
- Watch out for reptiles on the trail.

If you encounter any poisonous reptiles, like rattlesnakes, give them a wide berth and warn other hikers on the trail when you pass them. Despite the difficulty of Camelback Mountain, it is a magnificent hiking trail, and thousands of tourists come to Phoenix every year to climb it.

Desert Botanical Garden

If hiking Camelback Mountain seems too extreme for you, don't worry! There are plenty of other outdoor activities to try, including visiting the Desert Botanical Garden. A botanical garden might seem like an oxymoron, but there are actually more than 50,000 desert plants on show at this botanical garden (Desert Botanical Garden, n.d.).

The exhibit consists of local and imported desert plants, including cacti, trees, and flowers. There are also beautiful Chihuly glass sculptures. If you haven't seen Chihuly's work yet, it is all the more reason to visit the Desert Botanical Garden. The Desert Botanical Garden staff go to great lengths to ensure you have a pleasant experience at the garden. There are several 1.5-mile loop hiking trails that you can take to enjoy all the plants. Each trail is paved and easy to hike. The trails are also wheel-chair-friendly, making them accessible to everyone.

Children are welcome at Desert Botanical Garden and should enjoy the beautiful and interesting plants on display. There are strict rules against touching the plants, however. Children should be kept in check, so they don't damage the exhibitions.

In addition to the garden hiking trails, there are several special exhibitions yearly. Furthermore, you may see lectures and group tours taking place while you visit, which you are more than welcome to attend. Some festivals, like the Las Noches de las Luminarias, also occur throughout the year. Check the website before visiting Phoenix so you don't miss out on the fun.

There is a fee payable to enter the Desert Botanical Garden. Adults pay $25, while children aged 3-17 are charged $13. However, you can enter the Botanical Garden free of charge on Community Day, which occurs on the second Tuesday of every month. Bring a hat and sunscreen when visiting to protect yourself from the blazing Phoenix sun.

Oasis Water Park

If you visit Phoenix in summer, you will be no stranger to the desert heat. And in a place where water is scarce, a pool dip will be greatly welcomed after exploring the city on a summer's day. In this case, there is no better place to go than the Phoenix Oasis Water Park. The water park is located at the Arizona Grand Resort & Spa. Fortunately, the park is open to non-members, so you can enter even when not staying at the resort.

The water park offers fun water-based activities for everyone. "There is a wave pool for those who want to float on an inflatable, water slides for those looking for adventure, and a bubbling hot tub for those who aren't hot enough" (Lawrence, 2021).

The Oasis Wave Pool has swells of two feet, making it the perfect pool for small children and those who don't like rough waters. On the contrary, the water slides, known as Slide Canyon Tower, feature drops of 220 to 300 feet. While these slides are safe for all, they might not be your cup of tea. If these drops aren't quite thrilling enough, you can also try the Road Runner Slide, which features a 51-foot drop. That should set your heart racing.

The hot tub can hold up to 25 people and has soothing bubbles. This is the perfect spot to unwind those tight muscles after the Camelback mountain hike. Speaking of tight muscles, the resort also has massages and other spa treatments. You can enquire about these at the front desk or book them in advance on the website.

While access to the water park is free for those staying at the resort, day passes are available for those entering from outside the resort. A day pass costs $60 for adults and $55 for children (3-12). The day pass includes access to all the water slides and activities. The day pass also includes free parking and Wi-Fi. You can also reserve a pool chair at no extra charge.

Cabanas, spa treatments, and food and drinks are

charged separately. If you are heading to Phoenix, especially to visit the Oasis Water Park, I recommend staying at the Oasis Resort. Doing so gives you unlimited access to the water park and other amenities you would not otherwise have access to. Consult the website for prices for rooms and special packages.

Phoenix Zoo

The Phoenix Zoo is another spot perfect for family fun. The zoo is close to the Desert Botanical Garden and Papago Park, so you can easily visit these attractions in one day. However, I recommend going early in the day with Phoenix Zoo, as the Zoo gets quite busy. Furthermore, the animals are more active after breakfast and retreat into their sleeping dens in the hottest part of the day.

There are more than 3,000 animals to see at the Phoenix Zoo, including giraffes, elephants, monkeys, tigers, and zebras! Children and adults can also feed the giraffes at certain times during the day, making the zoo an interactive experience. There is also a petting zoo for the little ones, though adults are welcome there too.

Furthermore, the zoo has two water pads where children can cool off after playing in the sun. Access to the water pads is included in the admission fee. You can bring a cooler box with your food and drinks into the zoo. Glass bottles and alcohol are prohibited. There are eateries inside the zoo if you forget your cooler box at home.

Of course, there is a gift shop where you can buy

souvenirs and books about the Phoenix Zoo and other attractions around town. If you are tired from so much walking, you can hop on a safari cruiser tour. The tours are 25 minutes long and come with a narrated tour guide who shares information about the zoo and the animals.

Bring a hat and sunscreen when visiting, as you will be doing a lot of walking outside. There are three routes to walk in the zoo, with different animals and attractions along each route. The zoo is a fantastic experience for the whole family, especially if you don't have a zoo in your hometown. This is a fantastic experience to learn about animal conservation and to introduce your children to new animals.

Admission to the zoo is quite expensive, being $40 for adults and $30 for children (3-13). Many of the attractions at the zoo are also charged additionally, including feeding the giraffes and riding the carousel. You can save $5 per admission ticket by booking online. I highly recommend doing this as it also saves you time in the queue and grants you much quicker entry to the zoo.

Papago Park

Papago Park is another prime spot for taking pictures, exploring the desert, and relaxing with the family. The park is extremely rich in history. It was a reservation for the Native American tribes in the surrounding areas. It served as a POW camp during WWII, and houses the tomb of the first governor of Phoenix, George W.P. Hunt (Duran, 2019).

Papago Park is located near the Desert Botanical Garden and the Phoenix Zoo. If doing all three attractions, I recommend making Papago Park your final stop, as this park looks completely different at sunset. There are several easy hiking trails throughout the park, including:

- Hole-in-the-Rock Trail
- Papago Park Fitness Trail
- Crosscut Canal Path
- Double Butte Loop Trail
- Eliot Ramada Loop Trail

There are also several biking trails in the park. So, if you bring your off-road bikes, this park is the perfect spot to explore. The park sports several fishing ponds where you can enjoy an afternoon getting your lines wet.

Of course, one of the biggest attractions in Papago Park is the Hole in the Rock. Just a short 0.3-mile hike brings you to the viewpoint, where you can look out over downtown Phoenix, the Phoenix Zoo, and the sandstone formations in the park. You can even bring your four-legged best friend on this trail.

The Hole in the Rock was used to tell time by the Hohokam people who inhabited the area hundreds of years ago. Although Hole in the Rock is spectacular at any time of day, it is truly magical at sunset. But this is also when you can expect the most crowds in the park, as everyone shares this belief.

Entrance to the park is free, and there are plenty of things to see and do, so the entire family will enjoy the outing. Bring a hat, sunscreen, and sturdy walking shoes, as you will do a lot of walking in the park. Beware of wild animals, including lizards and rattlesnakes, in the park.

Pioneer Living History Museum

The Pioneer Living History Museum is the perfect spot to come if you want to combine a museum tour with an outdoor excursion. This field museum contains more than 30 original and recreated buildings and homes in the area. Some of the most notable buildings include "the Ashurst Cabin (the childhood home of Phoenix's first senator), a Teacherage cabin, and the flying "V" cabin, which belonged to a soldier during the last Apache war in 1882" (McKay, 2018).

You can see several recreated buildings, too, like a blacksmith shop, dress shop, and sheriff's office. Inside these stores, you can see artifacts from the era. You can enter the buildings, but don't touch any artifacts. Dangerous and fragile artifacts are caged in to prevent accidental breakage.

The field museum was erected in 1969 to show people what life was like in the late 1800s and early 1900s. The Living History Museum shares details of each home and building in the area. Special events occur on the sites, like gun fights and war reenactments. Consult the website before seeing if any such events are taking place—you wouldn't want to miss them.

Older children may enjoy learning about the history of Phoenix and Arizona. In contrast, the younger ones can explore the outdoors and enjoy gold panning or hay baling activities at the museum. The pathways are paved and broad enough for a stroller. There are also several park benches on the museum grounds for those needing a break.

Furthermore, there is a gift shop and eatery in the field museum. You can head there for lunch or dinner. Special guests may also perform on stage at the grill while you enjoy your meal. The Pioneer Living History Museum is intended for families, and there are activities for people of all ages to enjoy. However, this field museum is also popular for school field trips. Fortunately, school bookings are listed on the website's calendar. So, if you want to avoid school crowds, check on the website when school groups are scheduled to visit.

Entrance to the field museum is $12 for adults, $10 for children (5-16) or groups of 15 or more, and $8 for veterans. Remember to bring a hat, sunscreen, and comfortable shoes, as you will be doing plenty of walking at the Pioneer Living History Museum.

A Day In Phoenix

Considering all the great things you can do in Phoenix, visiting for only one day will certainly not be enough time to explore everything. However, a day is plenty of time to see some of Phoenix's attractions. It will make you appreciate the city more and give you a reason to return.

But what should you do if you only have one day in

Phoenix? Here is an example itinerary to make the most of your day in Phoenix.

Sunrise Hike at Hole in the Rock

Papago Park opens early enough for you to take the short hike to Hole in the Rock before sunrise. Hole in the Rock offers spectacular views of the entire area, including the Phoenix skyline and the Phoenix Zoo. A sunrise hike to Hole in the Rock ensures an even more impressive view, giving you an early start to the day.

An early hike at Papago Park can also turn into a morning spent fishing, biking, or exploring the rest of the area. So, if you have another day to spare in Phoenix, this might be the perfect way to spend it.

Stroll at Papago Park

Once you have admired the view from Hole in the Rock, why not take some time to explore the rest of Papago Park? There are so many interesting things to see, and you can even catch a fish in one of the pools. Papago Park is the perfect place to familiarize yourself with the Phoenix desert.

A stroll through the park gives you ample time to relax and appreciate the nature around you. If you are from the city and need some time to relax and reconnect with nature, this is the perfect place to do so. It is also the perfect place to bring your family if they have been stuck in a car for a few hundred miles.

Go to Desert Botanical Garden

After strolling through Papago Park, head to the Desert Botanical Garden next door to experience more of the beautiful plants growing in the desert. This is the perfect place for breakfast or lunch, giving you even more time outdoors. If you are in Phoenix to take pictures in the desert, the botanical garden is the place to be.

Don't forget to see if there are any special events, like the lights festival occurring, so you can plan your trip accordingly. There are many interesting things to witness at the Desert Botanical Garden, including the most spectacular glass sculptures.

Visit Arizona Science Center

When the clock strikes 12, and the sun is at its highest, it is a good idea to head inside and out of the heat. There is no better place to do this than at the Arizona Science Center. Here, you can have fun with all the interactive science exhibitions, learn about the stars and the galaxy, and watch a movie in the theater.

A trip to the Arizona Science Center also means you can explore downtown Phoenix. If you're feeling hungry after all your exploring, there is an eatery at the Science Center. Or you can choose from one of the many interesting restaurants located in downtown Phoenix for a truly unforgettable meal.

Hike Camelback Mountain

Finally, if you are still in need of fresh air, a late-afternoon hike to Camelback Mountain is the perfect way to end your day in Phoenix. Because of the difficulty of this trail, I recommend leaving the kids at home for this activity.

Camelback Mountain is one of the most popular hiking trails in the area, and it will undoubtedly give you a story to tell when you arrive home. While this trail is breathtaking at sunset, ensure you give yourself enough time to head back down before dark. Alternatively, bring a headlamp to help you navigate your way down the mountain.

Phoenix is the largest city in Arizona and has so many interesting things to do that mentioning them all seems impossible. But if you are looking for a road less traveled in Arizona and don't want to spend too much time in the city, there are also other places worth visiting, such as Sedona.

6

SEDONA

*S*edona *is a space of infinite creation in your heart, your greatest dream, and the most sacred moments of your life. And it is the power of your choice to choose hope even in the most difficult moments.* –Ilchi Lee

Sedona is another town with an interesting history in Arizona. Its origins are much more random than many other mining towns. And, yet, Sedona is one of the most recognizable places in the state. If you enjoy watching old western movies, chances are, you've seen one or two filmed in and around Sedona.

Despite being a small town, Sedona is still extremely popular among tourists, both from Arizona and out of state. But how did Sedona come to be, and what makes it such a famous town? To answer these questions, you must understand the history of Sedona and how it came to be.

A Little Bit of History

Like many other settlements in Arizona, Sedona was

home to Native American tribes long before any Europeans settled in the area. Tribes, such as Hohokam, Sinagua, and Anasazi, made an extraordinary living near Sedona. Despite the dry climate, they managed to farm with corn, beans, and squash. They also traded with neighboring clans.

Evidence of their presence is found in the impressive sandstone ruins around the area. But just like in many other areas in this guide, the Native Americans disappeared from the region without reason or explanation more than 500 years ago.

Thereafter, the area, which is now Sedona, lay uninhabited until the 1800s. "John James Thompson discovered Sedona while squatting in Oak Creek Canyon in 1876" ("History of Sedona," 2016). He saw the potential for farming and ranching and moved there with a few other families.

As more people heard of this remote farming location, they moved here to be more independent. By the early 1900s, nearly 30 families inhabited the area. In 1902, Theodore Schnelby petitioned for a post office, as the residents complained about how long their mail took to arrive ("History of Sedona," 2013). While Theodore initially proposed several names for the post office, all were rejected because they were too long. Eventually, he settled on naming the post office after his wife, Sedona, and so the town of Sedona was born.

Their primary income came from ranching and farming. But more impressively, peach and apple orchids were the driving force of Sedona's early economy. Farmers transported their fruit to neighboring towns, including Jerome, Phoenix, and Flagstaff. Sedona's fruit was so popular that people drove from Phoenix and other towns to buy some fresh fruit at the markets in Sedona.

As time progressed, more families moved into the area. They dug irrigation systems from Oak Creek to supply water to their orchids and lands. Interestingly enough, very few orchids remain in Sedona today, as the industry almost entirely disappeared by the 1980s.

Unlike many other boom towns in Arizona, Sedona remained a popular destination. This is partly thanks to the movie industry. Because of the impressive red rock formations around town, many filmmakers from Hollywood came here to shoot their Western movies. These movies ensured that Sedona would be the recognizable spot it is today.

Considering the town's interesting history, you might be interested in visiting, even if just to see where all the movies were made. But what is there to do and see in Sedona today? Let's find out.

Airport Mesa

One of the first attractions you should visit in Sedona is the Airport Mesa Lookout. The lookout point is conveniently located near Sedona Airport, making it an obvious choice as a first activity for those arriving in town via plane. From the Airport Mesa Lookout, you have a 360° view of Sedona and the surrounding valley.

You also have an unobstructed view of many impressive red rock formations surrounding Sedona, including Coffee Pot Rock, Cathedral Rock, Courthouse Rock, Bell Rock, and more. Airport Mesa is also one of Sedona's many vortex sites (sites with particular spiritual energies). Therefore, it is a popular spot for meditation and mindfulness.

There are two ways to reach the lookout point: hiking or driving. If you are keen on a hike, you can park at the trailhead and take the short, easy—but steep—hike to the lookout point. The trail is easy enough for almost anyone to complete, including children! However, it is a steep climb, and the rocks are slippery when wet, so it might not suit people with mobility problems.

Fortunately, you can also reach the lookout point by driving there. Drive past the trailhead and continue on the road until you reach the large parking space on your left. The best time to visit Mesa Airport Lookout is at dusk, as the sunlight reflects on the red sandstone rocks, turning the valley into a sparkly firepit. This is the most popular time to visit, so you will encounter a large crowd.

If you are an early riser, I recommend visiting the lookout point at dawn. The view is just as spectacular, and you won't have as many people competing for the perfect photo. There is a $3 parking fee at the trailhead and Lookout parking.

Amitabha Stupa and Peace Park

As mentioned, Sedona is a site with significant spiritual importance. According to many spiritual leaders, there is a powerful vortex in Sedona. A vortex is where spiritual energy flows—the more energy there flows, the more powerful the vortex. The vortex in Sedona invites people to receive healing, meditate, and find peace. Sedona is also a sacred site to the Native American tribes who roamed the area hundreds of years ago, as seen by the ruins they left behind.

Because of the spiritual power present in Sedona, many people from different religions travel here to pray, meditate, and receive healing from the vortex. And this is what inspired the Buddhist community to erect the Amitabha Stupa and Peace Park in town.

The Amitabha Stupa and Peace Park is a spiritual site you can reach through a short hiking trail. At the trail's end, you will reach the red Amitabha Stupa, which stands 36 feet tall and welcomes all the spiritual energy. You will also see a smaller Tara Stupa and a large wooden Buddha figure guarding the Peace Park.

Although Buddhists erected the site, and it has Buddhist artifacts, anyone is welcome to visit, regardless of religion. The Buddhists recognize this as a spiritual site and welcome anyone to pray and meditate here. You can make wishes, pray for healing, and thank the spirits for your blessings. The Peace Park is also a Wildlife sanctuary, so you may see some wild animals when hiking to the Stupas.

Even if you don't believe in vortexes and spiritual energy fields, the trail to the Amitabha Stupa is still an easy and enjoyable hike. The view from the Stupas is impressive, as are the artifacts and statues at the viewpoint. Be respectful of others when visiting, as they may be there to pray or meditate.

Although there aren't any age restrictions for visiting the Amitabha Stupa, I don't recommend bringing young children because they may be disruptive to other visitors. In addition, there aren't any activities for children, and they may not be interested in seeing the sculptures.

Entrance to the Amitabha Stupa is free. However, donations are always welcome as they help to maintain the site. You can speak to one of the workers or caretakers at the site if you want to make a donation or learn more about the Amitabha Stupa's history and significance.

Bell Rock

Of course, you cannot visit Sedona without hiking to one or more red sandstone rock formations that make the town so famous. One of the sandstone formations you should see is Bell Rock. Named so because of the shape of this formation, Bell Rock is a popular tourist attraction in Sedona.

The best way to experience the splendor of Bell Rock is to hike up to it. Several hiking trails in the area provide spectacular views of Bell Rock and the surrounding rock formations. The Bell Rock Loop Trail is a moderate hiking trail with many photo opportunities. "Depending on your path, the trail is between 0.8 and 1.5 miles long" (Nickerson, 2022). The trail consists of a gravel road that can take you to the summit of Bell Rock if you wish.

Although the hiking trail is moderately easy, it isn't

stroller friendly because of sections with steeper inclines and loose gravel. Fortunately, the trail is kid-friendly, provided your children have some hiking experience and wear proper clothing. Children younger than five may find the trail too difficult, so I recommend leaving the toddlers at home for this one.

Wear a hat, sunscreen, and proper hiking shoes when embarking on the Bell Rock Loop Trail. Some sections are nice and flat, while others are bumpy and filled with loose rocks, making it easy to lose your footing. However, if you are moderately fit, this trail should be an easy hike.

Because of how hot Sedona gets in summer, most people prefer to hike to Bell Rock just after dawn. It is cooler to hike the trail at this time, and the early sunlight also supplies the most breathtaking views. However, you may struggle with parking at the more popular hiking times. So, arrive as early as possible to avoid disappointment.

There is a park fee of $5 to hike to Bell Rock. This fee is for a day pass and grants you access to most hiking trails in the area—giving you even more reason to start your day early. You can purchase a pass at the machines, known as the "iron rangers," located at the trailhead.

Boynton Canyon

Boynton Canyon is another prime hiking trail for adventurers exploring Sedona. In addition to hiking up to the Boynton Canyon lookout, you can also take the Boynton Vista Trail, which takes you to the lookout of the impressive red rock formations. Furthermore, you can take the Subway Cave Trail, which leads you to some

Sinagua ruins in the caves of the surrounding mountains.

Both these trails are loops on the Boynton Canyon Trail, meaning you can hike to all three viewpoints in a single day. "The Boynton Canyon Trail is 6.3 miles long, while the total length of the hike when adding the other loops is 7.5 miles" (Julie, 2021). Hiking to all three attractions should take five to six hours, depending on how much time you take at each stop.

The Boynton Canyon Trail is an easy hiking trail, while the Boynton Vista and Subway Cave Trails are rated for moderate difficulty. That said, older children should have no difficulty completing all these trails, as they don't have steep climbs or particularly difficult sections.

Bring plenty of water on the trail, especially when hiking in summer. There isn't a lot of shade on the trail, and the summer temperatures can skyrocket in the middle of the day. Also, bring a hat, sunscreen, and sunglasses. You will need sturdy walking shoes for this trail, especially when hiking the Subway Cave Trail. If you have trouble with steep climbs, a walking stick will also be a great help on this trail, as there is a steep and slippery section before you reach the cave ruins.

Although the hiking trails are generally easy, the Subway Cave Trail involves scrambling between two rock formations, then creeping along the side of a rock face before reaching the caves. This section might not be suitable for small children or those who fear heights.

You require a pass to hike the Boynton Canyon Trail. A day pass is $5, and a week pass is $15. You can get either pass at the machines at the trailhead, which grant you access to most hiking trails around Sedona.

Cathedral Rock

Cathedral Rock is another unique red rock formation worth visiting. Several hiking trails take you to the rock formation, but the most direct route is the Cathedral Rock Trail. "This 1.3-mile out-and-back trail is moderately difficult and should take around two hours to complete" (Julie, 2021). Although the trail is short, there are some steep sections where you must scramble with your hands and feet over the rocks.

Other than that, the trail is manageable for anyone moderately fit. The best time to hike the Cathedral Rock Trail is at sunrise and sunset when the sunlight transforms the rock formations into glowing towers. The view from Cathedral Rock is absolutely breathtaking at this time, and you will have the opportunity to take the best photos.

Of course, these times are also popular for other hikers, so you will encounter crowds on the trail and at the lookout points. Parking at the trailhead also becomes a challenge at these times, which is why I recommend heading to the trail earlier rather than later. If hiking the Cathedral Rock Trail before sunrise or after sunset, bring a headlamp to navigate the rough terrain and steeper sections.

In addition to a headlamp, wear sturdy hiking shoes, a hat, and sunscreen. Bring plenty of water, and follow the "pack-it-in, pack-it-out" rules of hiking. Despite the challenging sections of this hiking trail, older children can easily complete it. Children younger than six may have trouble with the steeper sections. This trail is also not suitable for strollers or carriers.

There is a lookout point with a drop to the left side at the Cathedral Rock Lookout point. If you are afraid of heights or have younger children with you, I recommend staying clear of this point. It does make for great photos, however.

Like most other hiking trails in Sedona, you require a Red Rock Hiking Pass for the Cathedral Rock Trail. You can purchase this pass at the machines located at the trailhead for $5 per person. You can also hike this trail with an America the Beautiful Hiking Pass.

Slide Rock State Park

If you want to spend more time outside in Sedona, but the hiking trails are too much for the family, consider heading to Slide Rock State Park for some fun activities. There is a huge, natural slip-and-slide or water slide formed by the red sandstone in the area. "This State Park opened in 1987, though the land belonged to an apple farmer, Frank Pendley, who came here in 1907" (Brahan, 2022). Frank created an irrigation system from Oak Creek to irrigate his apple orchids.

When visiting Slide Rock State Park, you can still walk through the orchids and past the original farmhouse, packing shed, and tourist cabins. There are several activities to do in the park, including apple picking and bird and wildlife watching.

You can also explore one of several hiking trails through the mountains in the park. Of course, most people come to the park to see the Rock Slide at the creek. You can slide down this natural rockslide into Oak Creek and enjoy the day splashing in the river.

There are ponds with trout where you can spend the afternoon trying your luck with a fishing rod. There are also picnic tables and grills beside the pond where you can cook your freshly caught trout.

No luck catching a fish? Don't worry. A small, seasonal market in the park is open every day where you can buy supplies and snacks. The market is close to the rockslide and sells ice and souvenirs.

Bring water, food, sunscreen, and a hat to the park. I also recommend an extra pair of clothes for after going down the slide. The stone surface and algae may ruin your first set, so wear something you don't mind getting dirty. The park is intended for families, so it is ideal for children and seniors. Keep a close eye on young children at the creek, though, as the rocks are slippery, and the water is sometimes choppy. There aren't any lifeguards on duty. I recommend bringing some water shoes to protect your feet on the rocks. You can also bring a pool noodle or floatation device to relax in the creek.

There is a park entry fee of $20 per vehicle in the high season and $10 per vehicle in the low season (November to February).

A Day in Sedona

Given how many wonderful things there are to see and experience in Sedona, spending only one day in town seems impossible. However, if that is all the time you have, you should strive to make the most of it. Fortunately, you can still get plenty done in one day. Here is an example itinerary for the perfect day in Sedona.

Drive Red Rock Scenic Byway

If you only have a day in Sedona, there is no way you can hike all the trails in the area. Fortunately, there are several driving trails to follow that take you to some of the best lookout points in town.

The Red Rock Scenic Byway trail is one of those driving trails. It takes you to Cathedral Rock and Bell Rock while allowing you to marvel at the red rock formations Sedona is known for. While it isn't the same as hiking, it still allows you to admire the scenery and the famous attractions. Of course, it also takes a fraction of the time and is perfect for the whole family.

Walk the Bell Rock Pathway

If you have time for a hike, I recommend the Bell Rock hiking trail after the scenic drive. This short hiking trail gives you a glimpse of Sedona's wildlife and nature. It also takes you to one of the most famous rock formations in the area, allowing for an excellent photo opportunity.

Try to get on the trail as early as possible to avoid the crowds and leave you with enough time to explore other areas. Doing this trail early also means you get to see the sunrise over the rock formations, which is a truly spectacular sight.

Visit Slide Rock State Park

There is no better way to spend your afternoon in Sedona than by visiting Slide Rock State Park. Here, you will experience a bit of Sedona's past when walking through the apple orchids and past the farmhouse.

You can also swim in Oak Creek, catch fish in the pond, and pick apples from an orchid over 100 years old. This is the perfect picnic spot for lunch. If you have more than one day in Sedona, I strongly recommend setting aside at least half a day for Slide Rock State Park. There are so many things to explore here that an hour or two is barely enough to scratch the surface.

Go to the Viewpoint at Airport Mesa

Finally, you cannot leave Sedona without seeing the valley's view from the Airport Mesa lookout point. Arrive early enough to find parking and get ready to have your mind blown by the spectacular rock formations and town skyline view. You can drive or hike to the viewpoint, giving you a 360° view of Sedona.

Sedona is the perfect destination in Arizona for those who enjoy hiking, taking photos, and spending time outdoors. I strongly recommend spending at least a day in Sedona, Arizona, before heading to your following location. Where might that be? If your next stop is Tucson, keep reading! The next chapter will help you discover what awaits you in this city.

7

TUCSON

T here's something wonderfully healing in Arizona air.
–Zane Grey
          Tucson is another Arizonan city with a
fascinating history. "It is the second-largest city in Arizona
today, with a population of 542,629 in 2020" ("Tucson,"
2023). But of course, Tucson didn't always have the population it does today, nor was it such a peaceful city.

There are many battles, hijackings, and occupations in
Tucson's history, which will give you a better idea of why
the city today is the way it is. Fortunately, that is all in the
past. So, before familiarizing yourself with all the great
activities there are in Tucson, let's first consider its history.

A Little Bit of History

Tucson is the oldest incorporated city in Arizona. Like
many other cities and towns in the state, there is clear

evidence of Native American presence in the area long before Westerners arrived and developed it into a town. The Santa Cruz River, which flows past Tucson, provided Indian tribes, like the Hohokam people, with the resources needed to farm the lands. They created irrigation systems from the area to their fields, where they planted corn, legumes, and squashes.

By all accounts, the Native American tribes bordering the Santa Cruz River should have flourished. And yet, their sudden disappearance in the valley around 1100 remains a mystery. Nevertheless, "the area known today as Tucson was rediscovered in 1692 by a Spanish missionary who built a mission valley in 1700" ("Tucson," 2023). Soon after the mission, a military fort was built in the valley. The fort was named Presidio San Agustín del Tucsón, so the town of Tucson was born. Since their arrival in the valley, the Spanish fought constant battles against the Apache clans. However, these battles would not cease until long after the Spanish had left.

In 1821, after Mexico gained independence from Spanish rule, Tucson became a part of Mexico. American Mormons briefly conquered Tucson between 1846 and 1848, when the Mormons set upon building a railway to California. However, the Mormons never assumed control of the fort or the village, and the Mexican military never left the village at that time.

In 1854, Tucson officially became a part of the United States of America when America purchased the area now known as Arizona from Mexico during the Gadsden Purchase. Shortly after, a military fort was built at Tucson to guard the railway and ensure peace. Battles against the Apache Indians continued all this time.

After Arizona was recognized as a territory in 1863, more people moved there. It remained the state's military headquarters. "Tucson was incorporated in 1877, making it the oldest city in Arizona" ("Early Tucson," n.d.). The Santa Cruz River continued to make farming possible. Pomegranates, legumes, corn, squash, and pears constituted the largest portion of the farming industry.

Many people stopped by Tucson on their way to California. While it was already a large city at the time, Tucson very much instilled the idea of the wild west. Several famous gunfights and train robberies occurred near the town. However, the military force remained strong to protect the citizens and visitors on their way elsewhere.

Shortly after WWI, Tucson saw an influx of war veterans. Many had lung conditions because of the gas bombs used during the war and came to the desert for lung therapy. Several tuberculosis patients also sought relief in Tucson because of its hot, dry air. Tucson's climate is still ideal for those with lung conditions, as the dry climate provides relief from various health conditions.

Although Tucson is no longer the largest city in Arizona, it still sees more than seven million visitors annually. Why is this? What are all these people coming to the desert to see? Let's find out.

Catalina State Park

Catalina State Park is the perfect place to explore the desert and experience what it must have been like when the first settlers arrived. There are plenty of fun activities to do in the park. Where the Catalina State Park is now, there used to be one of the earliest cattle ranches in the area, known as Rancho Romero. "Francisco Romero, the grandson of a Spanish settler, apparently bought the property in 1844" (Walker, n.d.).

The property changed ownership over the next hundred years. Today, it is home to one of the best State Parks around Tucson. The park sees many visitors annually, as there is a lot to keep busy with. Hiking, biking, and horse riding are some of the most popular activities in the park.

The hiking trails vary from easy to extremely difficult. Loop trails occur throughout the park and in the surrounding foothills. Several trails also suit biking, so remember to bring your gear. Furthermore, horse stables are in the park, so you can bring your horse and go on an outride. If you don't have a horse, you can also go on one of the organized trail rides in the park. Visit the equestrian center for more information about the trail rides.

Many people also come to Catalina State Park for bird watching—more than 150 bird species live there. Of course, the scenery is also spectacular, with many desert plants to observe. Picnic tables and grills are also in the park, making it the perfect spot for a day filled with fun and adventure. Don't forget to see the Romero pools for an afternoon dip or photo session.

Catalina State Park is perfect for the family. Many of the trails are easy enough to do with kids. A discovery center is also located at the ranger station at the park's entrance. Of course, kids between six and twelve can also receive their junior ranger badges at Catalina State Park— enquire about this program on arrival.

You can also stay in the park to explore more of the trails. 120 Camping spots are in the camp. Each spot has running water, an electricity port, a grill, a picnic bench, and a bathroom. Those with an RV can also use one of the RV spots. Camping is on a first-come-first-serve basis. Those bringing horses may leave them in one of the pens at the equestrian center for no charge.

Entrance to the park is charged at $7 per vehicle (4 adults) and $3 per pedestrian or cyclist entering. Contact the park to enquire about the status of the hiking trails or special events before arrival. Some camping spots may also be charged additionally. You can enquire about their availability at the visitor center too.

Colossal Cave Mountain Park

The Colossal Cave Mountain Park is another park suited to those who enjoy hiking and horseback riding. The mountain park has three caves to explore: the Colossal Cave, the La Tarjeta Cave, and the Arkenstone Cave. The Colossal Cave is the most popular tourist destination. Daily guided tours can take you to the cave as the tour guide shares the cave's history, scientific facts, and other fascinating details. The trail to the cave is a short, half-mile walk. You don't need special equipment for the trail, though I recommend wearing comfortable shoes with sufficient grip.

The rest of Colossal Cave Mountain Park is just as enjoyable. There are several other hiking trails and horse riding trails. You can find more information about the guided horse riding tours at the equestrian center. Picnic tables at the park make it the perfect stop for an afternoon adventure. For those interested in learning more about the history of the park and surrounding area, you can visit the La Posta Quemada Ranch Museum and the Civilian Conservation Corps Museum, both located on park grounds.

Colossal Cave Mountain has a fascinating history. Before becoming a state park, it was a ranch, resort, conservationist site, and hideout for bandits and criminals. You can find out more about this history at the museums. There is also a visitor center and gift shop where you can buy trinkets and souvenirs to remind you of your time in Tucson.

Although the Colossal Cave allows children over five, I recommend leaving them behind for this tour. There are sheer drops when you enter the cave, and the safety railings don't provide enough safety for younger children who may fall over or slip. Fortunately, another cave adventure is specially designed with the young ones in mind. The Toddler Time Tours are designed for young children.

These half-hour tours are safe, fun, and informational for toddlers and children.

You can find more information about these tours at the visitor center. The park also has a beautiful butterfly garden where you can take children to watch the annual butterfly migration and other animals in the garden. Unfortunately, colossal Cave Mountain Park is more expensive than other attractions in the area. Admission for the Colossal Cave Tour is $22 for adults and $12 for children (5-12).

Saguaro National Park

Saguaro National Park is yet another park worth exploring around Tucson. This park is home to the infamous saguaro cactus, a cactus species which only grows in the Sonoran desert. "These cacti can grow over 70 feet tall and live more than 200 years" (Carlson, 2022). Therefore, the Saguaro National Park is the perfect place to photograph these cacti in their full glory and explore the surrounding area.

The park is divided into Rincon Mountain District (the eastern section) and Tucson Mountain District (the western section). Each district is unique, and if you have enough time, I recommend stopping at both. The Tucson Mountain District has a denser population of saguaro cacti, making it a more popular tourist destination. You can take beautiful photos of the cacti and surrounding area when visiting this side of the park. The eastern side, on the contrary, has fewer saguaros. It also has fewer tourists. However, what makes this side unique is the fact that there are outback camping sites. So, if you plan to spend more than a day at Saguaro National Park, this is where you will head for your first night.

The camping spots aren't accessible by car, so you must hike to reach them. There aren't any amenities at the campsite, so bring what you need. While the campsites are not for the faint of heart, it is a once-in-a-lifetime experience to camp in the Sorano desert under the stars.

The Saguaro National Park also has other hiking trails, biking trails, and lookouts to visit. One of the top tourist attractions in the park is the Petroglyphs. "These rock paintings were made by the Hohokam people who lived in the area a thousand years ago" (Julie, 2023). You can find the Petroglyphs at Signal Hill on the Baja Loop Trail. This trail is accessible to vehicles, so you don't have to hike there.

Furthermore, there are self-guided tours with information plaques sharing information about the desert and the saguaro cacti. These plaques are found on the Desert Discovery Nature Trail. Most trails in the park are easy enough for children to accompany you.

Of course, there are also some fun activities for the juniors, including the junior ranger program. Enquire about the program at any of the park's visitor centers. The center's guides will also share information about the park, including closed-off roads, flash flood risks, etc.

A day pass for Saguaro National Park is $25 for a private vehicle and $15 per individual entering the park. You can also obtain an annual pass for the park, which costs $45. You need a permit for camping in Saguaro National Park, which you can buy online for $8 per person. There are various campsites throughout the park. Enquire at the visitor center about the condition of each campsite and potential camp closures due to weather conditions.

Mt. Lemmon Scenic Byway

The Mt. Lemmon Scenic Byway is something you must see on Mt. Lemmon Scenic Byway before leaving Tucson. Mt. Lemmon is unique in that the elevation gain allows plants and trees to grow there that would otherwise not survive the desert heat. The Scenic Byway is a driving road, but you can also hike or cycle up to the summit if you want to. There are several hiking trails along the byway. As you drive up, you will notice how the saguaros and desert sand give way to other plants, including pine trees.

Because of the elevation, it's important to pack for all weather conditions. Temperatures at the summit differ significantly from those in Tucson. You may even see snow and go skiing at the summit. There are picnic areas along the trail where you can stop for lunch, but there aren't any restaurants or shops until you reach the top. "If you pull off for a picnic, you must have a park permit, as Mt. Lemmon Byway is a part of Coronado National Forest" (Ray, 2022). You can purchase a park permit at one of the machines along the route for $8.

The National Forest also has many hiking trails and

some camping spots if you wish to overnight on your journey to the summit. These camping sites offer magnificent photo opportunities, allowing you to experience this unique biome in more detail.

The byway has few activities; you will mostly drive up to the summit. However, you can experience some of the most magnificent views you have ever seen. And, because you won't have to walk, this is the perfect activity for those who cannot walk because of mobility issues or families with small children. The drive up and down is spectacular any time of day. Still, the mountain transforms into a pink and orange canvas at sunset, the most popular time to drive up to Mt. Lemmon's summit.

Unfortunately, hikers and cyclists should aim to go up early in the day, as you need an entire day to hike up and down the mountain. In addition, you need plenty of sunlight to navigate the terrain. Several restaurants, gift shops, and activities are at the top of Mt. Lemmon. Most hikers hike the Marshall Gulch Trail at the top, a loop trail that takes them to the summit of Mt. Lemmon. As you can imagine, the view from the summit is spectacular.

Old Tombstone Western Theme Park

The Old Tombstone Western Theme Park is the ideal spot to spend the day learning about life in Tucson and the surrounding areas at the turn of the century. This theme park is based on the historical buildings and layout of Old Tombstone, a suburb of Tucson. The theme park offers something for everyone, from watching a hilarious gunfight reenactment to panning for gold.

A trolly takes you on tour through the town, and there are also ghost and murder tours on some nights. You can take a picture behind bars at the jail or learn more about Tombstone's history while playing a round of mini golf. After all the hiking you have done in Tucson, why not take a ride in one of the horse-drawn carriages around town?

Old Tombstone Western Theme Park is a family theme park, so you can rest assured that all activities, except the ghost tours, are suitable for children of all ages. Stop at the Cantina for Western-style food or an ice-cold beer after a long day. While the theme park shares some of the area's history, and the gunfights are historically accurate and based on actual fights, don't expect a complete history lesson of the area.

Tombstone Western Theme Park is meant to be a fun activity and therefore isn't as focused on the town's history as a museum. Instead, you can expect to laugh and have fun while visiting the park. Entrance to the Theme Park is free, but you do need to book most of the activities inside, which comes at a cost.

- Tickets for the gunfight play are $10 for adults and $8 for children (5-12).
- Tickets for the trolley tour are $15 for adults and $10 for children.
- Tickets for the Ghost and Murder trolley tour are $25 for adults and $20 for children (no children under five allowed).

Consult the website for special prices and limited-time activities at the Old Tombstone Western Theme Park. Don't forget to bring a hat, sunscreen, water, and comfortable shoes.

Seven Falls

Another excellent activity in Tucson is hiking the Seven Falls Trail. This 8.2-mile trail takes you to seven waterfalls, a strange occurrence in the desert. Surrounded by rocky mountains and cacti, the Seven Falls really is a striking scene. It is one of Tucson's most popular hiking trails, so be prepared to meet large crowds, especially on weekends.

The best time to hike Seven Falls is early in spring. This gives you the best chance to see water as the snowy ice caps begin to melt. The temperatures are also more moderate than in the winter. If you are in Tucson in summer, you may not see any water at the falls. In addition, Tucson's summer temperatures are known to be relatively high. So, if you plan to hike the Seven Falls Trail in the summer, I recommend getting an early start and bringing plenty of water. The Seven Falls Trail is in the Sabino Canyon Recreation area, a space with more than 30 hiking and biking trails and plenty of wildlife to admire.

There are two trailheads to choose from. The first is the Bear Canyon Trailhead. This trail is a 6.8-mile roundtrip. Although the trail is rated as easy, the steep incline may make it difficult for some. This trail is certainly accessible for children with prior hiking experience or reasonable fitness.

The other trailhead is at the Sabino Canyon Recreation Area parking lot. You can start your hike directly at the trailhead or hop onto one of the shuttles that take you part of the way. From the trailhead, the hike is about 8.3 miles out and back. However, the hike is only 3.6 miles long if you take the shuttle. Just like the Bear Canyon Trailhead, the Sabino Canyon Trailhead is an easy hike and can accommodate the whole family. If your kids are too small to walk the entire way, I recommend using the shuttle service.

Bring comfortable hiking shoes, water, a hat, and sunscreen on the trail. Remember to bring a swimsuit if you plan to swim at the waterfalls. Because this hike is easy to moderate, you don't need any special equipment. However, note that there are some steeper sections on the trail. It is best to start the hike at sunrise, as this will give you plenty of time to spend at the waterfalls and return without hiking in the dark.

Unfortunately, if you take the shuttles, you won't have such an early start as they only start transporting people at 09:15. You will also encounter many more people when using the shuttles. You need a permit to enter the park and hike to Seven Falls. Day passes are available for $8 per vehicle. An America the Beautiful pass is also acceptable for this trail. Shuttle fees from Sabino Canyon Recreation Area's parking lot are an additional fee of $6 per adult and $4 per child (3-12).

Tucson Mountain Park

Tucson Mountain Park is yet another prime spot to experience the saguaros at their best. With several hiking trails, camping areas, and bird-watching opportunities, Tucson Mountain Park is the perfect place to relax and get to know the Sorano desert. The visitor center at the park's entrance offers a checklist for all bird watchers (Tucson Mountain Park, n.d.). So, pack your binoculars and watch the horizon when exploring the park.

The picnic areas in the park offer the perfect place for lunch after hiking some trails. Be mindful of your surroundings while enjoying your picnic. Wild animals, like rattlesnakes, are prominent in the park. Always follow the "pack-it-in, pack-it-out" principle when hiking or spending time in the park. Speaking of hiking, there are several hiking trails around Tucson Mountain Park. Some hiking trails are more strenuous, but many trails are also suitable for children. Some of the best hiking trails for children in Tucson Mountain Park are:

- Brown Mountain Trail
- Hidden Canyon Bowen Loop Trail
- Yetman and Rock Wren Trail
- Camaro Loop Trail
- Golden Gate Trail, and Ironwood Trail

Despite being some of the easier trails in Tucson Mountain Park, they still offer plenty of beautiful sites and are difficult enough to break out a sweat. Wear sturdy hiking shoes and a hat when hiking. Bring enough water and watch out for wildlife while hiking. The best time to visit Tucson Mountain Park for hiking is in spring and fall when the weather is more moderate.

If one day in the park is not enough, you can also stay overnight at one of the campsites. Gilbert Bay Camping Terrain is located inside Tucson Mountain Park. It offers 130 campsites, five of which are for tents only. Each campsite has water, a toilet, a table, and a grill for charcoal fires only. There are no shower amenities on the campsite. You can make a reservation in advance when going to Tucson Mountain Park, and I recommend doing so during the busier season (November to April).

Entering Tucson Mountain Park requires no park fees, but you may have to pay for overnight camping. You can enquire more about this on their website or at the visitor center.

A Day in Tucson

Although getting anything done in Tucson in just one day seems nearly impossible, you may be surprised to see just how much you can explore in 24 hours. Unfortunately, there isn't enough time for an overnight stay in one of the parks, but one day is still plenty to experience some great activities and scenery Tucson offers. So, what should you do with only one day in Tucson?

Visit Barrio Viejo

Barrio Viejo in downtown Tucson offers you a peek into the brightly colored adobe-style houses. Walking in

Barrio Viejo will give you a sense of the Spanish and Mexican lifestyle of the 1800s.

"Barrio Viejo means "old neighborhood" in Spanish" (Travelingness, 2022). Barrio Viejo will give you the perfect photo opportunities and allow you to delve into the past. It also offers you the opportunity to explore the downtown area of Tucson, which is a unique opportunity on its own. Many hidden gems are found in the downtown area.

Eat Mexican Food

Tucson is famous for its Mexican food, and many people believe that the city has the best Mexican cuisine in all of Arizona. So, after working up an appetite while walking through the city, why not stop for a taco or a classic Mexican feast?

You will find a Mexican restaurant around every corner, each offering a meal as delicious as the next. While the entire city has countless Mexican restaurants to choose from, rumor has it that the best—and cheapest— Mexican cuisine is found in downtown Tucson.

View the Murals Around the City

While you are downtown, don't forget to admire some famous murals around the city. Tucson murals are a blend of Mexican-style art and Western art. Downtown Tucson is full of murals and street art, offering more photo opportunities. So, you can explore the art scene in Tucson before and after enjoying some of the best food in town.

Visiting downtown Tucson is also fun if you run low on funds, as you can see all these wonderful things at no

cost. Remember to watch out for any other unique opportunities that may present themselves in the area.

Go to Saguaro National Park

Finally, you cannot leave Tucson without stopping at
the Saguaro National Park and experiencing the saguaros
standing tall. The Saguaro National Park has plenty of
hiking trails, driving trails, and, of course, viewpoints to
admire the tall saguaro cacti.

Informational plaques tell you more about the
saguaro cacti and their origins. Heading into the park to
see the sunset is the perfect way to end your day in
Tucson. If you have more time in Tucson, I recommend
setting aside at least half a day for the Saguaro National
Park. There is so much to do that a few hours will never
seem enough.

Arizona has so much more to offer than a trip to the
Grand Canyon. From seeing the ghost towns and sliding
jails around Jerome to taking on several hiking trails in
the mountains and valleys, Arizona is the perfect destination for anyone looking for a new place to go on their next
holiday. Arizona is peaceful, eventful, and freeing. It is the
perfect destination for those looking for a new adventure.

AFTERWORD

After reading this guide, you should know what Arizona offers besides the Grand Canyon. Of course, visiting the Grand Canyon is a wonderful experience and a trip you should definitely make when in Arizona. However, Arizona offers so much more than just the Grand Canyon.

Traveling through Arizona state will give you a newfound respect for life in the 1800s and 1900s. You will gain insight into what the pioneers saw when they first arrived in Arizona, what the Native Americans fought so hard to protect, and what the US government now works so hard to maintain. The average family has so much on their plate. Some have a family to care for, a job they work hard at, and a long-term ambition to explore her country and other countries around the world.

Arizona is among the best states to visit. Whether traveling alone, with your family, or with your friends, you will surely find something fun to experience in Arizona.

Why not see what else Arizona offers other than the Grand Canyon?

After reading this guide, you will have a great idea of what else there is to do in Arizona. Though there are many more places to explore, these seven towns and cities are a great start to inspire your Arizona holiday.

Flagstaff

Being one of the first cities you come across in Arizona from the Grand Canyon, you will quickly realize what the first pioneers saw in this location and why they settled here to establish Flagstaff. Flagstaff has plenty to offer; some of the top things tourists come to Flagstaff to see are:

- The Arizona Snowbowl
- Coconino Lava River Cave
- Lowell Observatory
- Museum of Northern Arizona
- Riordan Mansion State Historic Park
- Route 66
- Sunset Crater Volcano
- Walnut Canyon National Monument
- Wupatki National Monument

Flagstaff is the ideal location for those wanting to learn more about Arizona's history and who enjoy hiking and exploring the wilderness. Whether it's your first or last stop in Arizona, you will surely have a memorable experience, nonetheless.

Williams

The next stop, and in my opinion, one of the most tourist-worthy destinations in the guide, is Williams. Williams started at a small railway construction camp but soon grew in popularity as people visited the Grand Canyon via train departing from Williams. At Williams, you will experience:

- Raptor Ranch Birds of Prey
- Sycamore Falls
- Grand Canyon Railway
- Bearizona Wildlife Park
- Route 66
- Kaibab National Forest

Williams has a little something for everyone. It is undoubtedly the best place to head if you want an authentic experience at the Grand Canyon. This town is perfect for anyone—solo travelers, families, or friends.

Jerome

Visiting Jerome will give you a great idea of how resilient Arizona's first settlers were. Built against a mountain, Jerome stares out over the Verde Valley. There are plenty of interesting attractions to witness in Jerome. In addition to the spectacular scenery, tourists flock to Jerome to experience the following:

- Jerome State Historic Park
- The Sliding Jail
- Jerome Ghost Tours
- Gold King Mine and Ghost Town

Jerome made its success off the copper mines in the surrounding area. And although it was heading to full ghost town status for a few decades, it is now a flourishing artist destination. Jerome is perfect for those with an interest in Arizona's mining history and ghost towns.

Page

Page can truly be named an oasis in the desert. This town exists today because of the construction of the Glen Canyon Dam in the 1950s and 1960s. It is one of the newest towns in Arizona. And although Page has few permanent residents, it sees plenty of tourists annually who travel here to witness the dam and other attractions. This is where most tourists go who come to Page:

- Antelope Canyon
- Glen Canyon Dam
- Lake Powell
- Horseshoe Bend
- Grand Staircase-Escalante National Monument
- Vermillion Cliffs National Monument

A trip to Page will inform you just how much technology has helped us. The Glen Canyon Dam supplies water to Page and many cities and towns in the surrounding area. Thanks to the engineers and investors, many of these places still exist. Page is the perfect place to marvel at human inventions and enjoy the water activities at Lake Powell.

Phoenix

Phoenix is the capital of Arizona and also has the biggest population. As such, it would be a shame to travel to Arizona without stopping in its capital. Although some of the smaller towns offer a unique charm and glimpse into the past, Phoenix is all about the future. A trip to Phoenix allows you to visit:

- Arizona Capitol Museum
- Arizona Science Center
- Camelback Mountain
- Desert Botanical Garden
- Oasis Water Park
- Phoenix Zoo
- Papago Park
- Pioneer Living History Museum

Phoenix is a great blend of the old and the new. It is the perfect family destination. However, if you are going on a solo trip or a trip with friends, you may also find various attractions to enjoy. You would need at least two days to explore Phoenix—one day for downtown Phoenix and another for the surrounding areas.

Sedona

Sedona is a city with a fascinating history. It doesn't owe its origins to mining or farming, and yet it is still one of the most recognizable places in all of Arizona. Because of its unique mountainous surroundings, Sedona was the prime location for Western movies in the late 20th century. A trip to Sedona will show you:

- Airport Mesea
- Amitabha Stupa and Peace Park
- Bell Rock
- Boynton Canyon
- Cathedral Rock
- Slide Rock State Park

If you enjoy hiking and photography, Sedona is the perfect spot for a getaway. It will help you reconnect with nature, find your spiritual self, and gaze at the beauty of nature and the adaptiveness of the Native American tribes who lived here hundreds of years ago.

Tucson

Tucson is another city with an interesting past. Today, it may be the second largest city in Arizona, but it was actually a long time before people started settling in the area.

Tucson has many interesting features, including its occupational history. When visiting Tucson, you will see:

- Catalina State Park
- Colossal Cave Mountain Park
- Saguaro National Park
- Mt. Lemmon Scenic Byway
- Old Tombstone Western Theme Park
- Seven Falls
- Tucson Mountain Park

Tucson is a great place to visit if you enjoy hiking, being outside, and visiting historic places. Whether it's with the family or alone, Tucson will surely be an enjoyable experience. Don't forget to set aside a day to explore downtown Tucson and eat some authentic Mexican cuisine.

After living in Arizona for a long time, I am so excited to share this knowledge with all my readers. I hope the cities and places I have shared with you in this guide are enough to convince you to visit this wonderful state. It is time to choose a location and get exploring! With this book as your guide, you will gain a greater appreciation and love of Arizona as you witness its beauty and wonder firsthand.

If you enjoyed this book, I would greatly appreciate it if you could write a review. I cannot express how much joy it brings me to read your thoughts on my work and to see how many people I have inspired to visit Arizona. Happy traveling!

BIBLIOGRAPHY

About The Mountain. (n.d.). Arizona Snowbowl. https://www.snow-bowl.ski/the-mountain/mountain-information/

About – Hotel Monte Vista. (n.d.). Hotelmontevista. https://hotelmonte-vista.com/about/

Arizona Science Center - Phoenix AZ, 85004. (n.d.). Visit Phoenix https://www.visitphoenix.com/listing/arizona-science-center/54/

Barks, C. (2020, September 28). *12 Tips For Successfully Hiking Camelback Mountain In Phoenix*. TravelAwaits. https://www.travelawaits.-com/2555260/tips-for-hiking-camelback-mountain/

Basecamp at Snowbowl. (n.d.). Discover Flagstaff. https://www.flagstaffari-zona.org/directory/basecamp-at-snowbowl/?gclid=CjwKCAiA3pugBh-AwEiwAWFzwdVKNkaZq4l44UyhpqHIg-CIb4di7hzpzLC-lVscpsVP9MjiIEGwhnBoCmV8QAvD_BwE

Best Kid Friendly Trails in Kaibab National Forest. (n.d.). All Trails. https://www.alltrails.com/parks/us/arizona/kaibab-national-forest/kids#:~:text=Where%20is%20the%20best%20kid,star%20rat-ing%20from%20297%20reviews

Best Kid Friendly Trails in Sunset Crater Volcano National Monument. (n.d.). All Trails. https://www.alltrails.com/parks/us/arizona/sunset-crater-volcano-national-monument/kids#:~:text=Accord-ing%20to%20users%20from%20AllTrails,star%20rat-ing%20from%20765%20reviews

Brahan, P. (2022, May 26). *Slide Rock State Park – What to See and Do. Just Go Travel Studios*. https://www.justgotravelstudios.com/blogs/just-go-travel-blog/slide-rock-state-park-arizona

The Brief History of the City of Page. (2001). Lake Powell. https://www.lake-powell.net/pagehistory.htm

Camelback Mountain. (n.d.). Visit Phoenix. https://www.visitphoenix.-com/sonoran-desert/parks/camelback-mountain/

Carlson, T. (2022, October 6). *What to do in Saguaro National Park with Kids*. Big Brave Nomad. https://www.bigbravenomad.com/blog/what-to-do-in-saguaro-national-park-with-kids

City of Page History. (n.d.). CityofPage. https://cityofpage.org/about-page/city-of-page-history

City of Phoenix History. (2019). Phoenix. https://www.phoenix.gov/pio/city-publications/city-history

Coconino National Forest - Lava River Cave. (2014). Usda. https://www.fs.usda.gov/recarea/coconino/recarea/?recid=55122

Cole, B. (2022, January 13). *Antelope Canyon with Kids: The Ultimate Guide to a Fun Family Visit.* Ouroffbeatlife. https://ouroffbeatlife.com/antelope-canyon-with-kids/

Desert Botanical Garden | Family Activities in Phoenix. (n.d.). Kid City Guide Phoenix. https://phoenix.kidcityguide.com/place/family-activities-in-phoenix/

Duran, D. (2019, June 26). *Your Complete Guide to Papago Park.* TripSavvy. https://www.tripsavvy.com/papago-park-phoenix-complete-guide-4582471

Early Tucson. (n.d.). Arizona Historical Society. https://arizonahistoricalsociety.org/education/esperanza/early-tucson/

Erika. (2018, June 8). The Grand Canyon Railway and Hotel: Is It Worth It? A SoCal Way of Life. https://asocalwayoflife.com/the-grand-canyon-railway-and-hotel-is-it-worth-it/

Facility Information | Jerome State Historic Park. (n.d.). Azstateparks. https://azstateparks.com/jerome/explore/facility-information

Family Fun Weekend Trip Williams and the Grand Canyon Travel Itinerary. (n.d.). Arizona Grand Canyon State. https://www.lamag.com/wp-content/uploads/sites/6/2015/04/travel-itinerary-williams-grand-canyon.pdf

Flagstaff, Arizona History. (n.d.). Discover Flagstaff. https://www.flagstaffarizona.org/things-to-do/arts-culture/history/

Frazer, K. (2019, April 27). *1 Day in Page, Arizona Itinerary | The best things to do in Page.* Adventures of A+K. https://adventuresofaplusk.com/1-day-in-page/

Fromm, E. (2020, September 7). *7 Incredible Things To Explore At Walnut Canyon National Monument.* TravelAwaits. https://www.travelawaits.com/2553900/things-to-explore-at-walnut-canyon-national-monument/

Fromm, E. (2022, May 5). *10 Reasons To Visit Sunset Crater Volcano National Monument.* TravelAwaits. https://www.travelawaits.com/2494613/sunset-crater-volcano-national-monument-reasons-to-visit/

Gagner, P. (2022, March 3). *The Wave Arizona: Everything you need to know.* Dreamlandtours. https://dreamlandtours.net/the-wave-arizona-everything-you-need-to-know/#:~:text=The%20Wave%20is%20a%20highly

Haveman, L. (2017, July 29). *Bearizona.* Phoenix with Kids. https://www.phoenixwithkids.net/bearizona/

Hiking for Kids in the Grand Staircase-Escalante National Monument, Utah. (n.d.). Zion National Park. http://www.zionnationalpark.com/gskids.htm

History of Flagstaff, Arizona. (2023, February 17). Wikipedia. https://en.wikipedia.org/wiki/History_of_Flagstaff,_Arizona

History of Sedona. (2013, March 24). Sedona Heritage Museum. https://sedonamuseum.org/historyofsedona/

History of Sedona: Learn About the First Settlers of Sedona. (2016, September 30). Andante Inn of Sedona. https://www.andanteinn.com/history-of-sedona-area/#:~:text=The%20first%20Europeans%2C%20a%20Spanish

Howell, W. (2016, January 5). *Out of the past: A brief history of Williams and 121 years of education (part 1 of 3).* Williams News. https://www.williamsnews.com/news/2016/jan/05/out-of-the-past-a-brief-history-of-williams-and-1/

Julie. (2019, June 24). *8 Amazing Things to do in Saguaro National Park.* Earth Trekkers. https://www.earthtrekkers.com/best-things-to-do-in-saguaro-national-park/

Julie. (2021a, April 18). *How to Hike Boynton Canyon & the Subway Cave | Sedona, Arizona.* Earth Trekkers. https://www.earthtrekkers.com/how-to-hike-boynton-canyon-subway-cave/

Julie. (2021b, April 24). *How to Hike to Cathedral Rock in Sedona, Arizona.* Earth Trekkers. https://www.earthtrekkers.com/how-to-hike-cathedral-rock-trail-sedona/

Kara. (2022, October 9). *5 Reasons You'll Love Bearizona Wildlife Park In Williams.* Karabou. https://thekarabou.com/bearizona-wildlife-park/

Lava Tubes | Lava River Caves. (n.d.). Flagstaff. https://www.flagstaff.com/lava-tubes

Lawrence, K. (2021, May 31). *Make A Splash This Summer At Arizona's Oasis Water Park, One Of The Top 10 Water Parks In The U.S. Only In Your State.* https://www.onlyinyourstate.com/arizona/oasis-water-park-az/

Lawrence, K. (2022, June 1). *There's An Old West Themed Amusement Park In Arizona And It's A Ghost Town Come To Life.* Only In Your State.

https://www.onlyinyourstate.com/arizona/themed-amusement-park-az/

LeBlanc, D. (n.d.). *Mount Lemmon Scenic Byway*. Outdoor Project. https://www.outdoorproject.com/united-states/arizona/mount-lemmon-scenic-byway#:~:text=The%20Mount%20Lemmon%20Scenic%20Byway

Lowell Observatory Flagstaff AZ. (n.d.). Flagstaff. https://www.flagstaff.com/lowell-observatory

Martinez, G. (n.d.). *Hike | Lava River Cave | Flagstaff. Arizona Hikers Guide.* http://www.arizonahikersguide.com/all-hikes/hike-lava-river-cave-flagstaff

McClellan, J. (2018, April 11). *Phoenix Zoo: What to know before you go. A helpful guide for families planning to visit.* The Arizona Republic. https://www.azcentral.com/story/entertainment/kids/2018/04/11/phoenix-zoo-know-before-you-go/1089059001/

McKay, P. (2018, October 5). *Pioneer Living History Museum*. Phoenix with Kids.   https://www.phoenixwithkids.net/pioneer-living-history-museum/

Melissa. (2022, May 23). *10 Best Flagstaff Hiking Trails*. The Modern Female Hiker. https://www.femalehiker.com/hikes/best-flagstaff-hiking-trails/

Morris, T. (2020, July 27). *Experiences*. Raptor Ranch. https://raptor-ranch.com/raptor-encounters/experiences/

Nardelli, F. (2017, June 2). *Glen Canyon Dam: Overlook, Tour, Hours, Admission Fee and Directions*. Travel in USA. https://www.travelinusa.us/glen-canyon-dam-lake-powell/

Nickerson, S. (2022, August 14). *Bell Rock Trail Loop for Young Kids - What to Expect and Bring*. Sengerson. https://www.sengerson.com/bell-rock-loop-trail-with-young-kids/#:~:text=Is%20Bell%20Rock%20trail%20in

Ockey, N. (2019, May 9). *Glen Canyon Dam*. Utah's Adventure Family. https://www.utahsadventurefamily.com/glen-canyon-dam/

Page Lake Powell Information. (n.d.). Powellguide. http://www.powellguide.com/lake_powell_info/john_wesley_powell_museum.htm

Pete's Route 66 Gas Station Museum, Williams. (n.d.). Cityseeker. https://cityseeker.com/williams-az/1327644-pete-s-route-66-gas-station-museum

Phoenix (mythology) - New World Encyclopedia. (n.d.). Newworldencyclopedia. https://www.newworldencyclopedia.org/entry/Phoenix

Ray. (2022, August 18). *Shaka Guide.* Shakaguide. https://www.shakaguide.-com/article/tucson/know-before-you-go-mt-lemmon-scenic-byway

Reshma. (2021, January 15). *195 Arizona Quotes to Inspire a Trip to the Stunning Copper State.* The Solo Globetrotter. https://thesologlobetrotter.-com/arizona-quotes-about-arizona/

Riordan Mansion State Historic Park. (2022, September 29). America's State Parks. https://www.americasstateparks.org/riordan-mansion-state-historic-park/

Riordan Mansion. (2022). Flagstaff. https://www.flagstaff.com/riordan-mansion

Robinson, K. (2021, January 14). *From Alice Cooper to Michael Phelps, these celebrities call metro Phoenix home.* The Arizona Republic. https://www.azcentral.com/story/entertainment/peo-ple/2021/01/14/celebrities-who-live-in-arizona/6600541002/

Rose, B. (2019, March 25). *Here's what you need to know before visiting the remote Grand Staircase-Escalante National Monument.* Roadtrippers. https://roadtrippers.com/magazine/visit-grand-staircase-escalante/

Rumbley, K. (n.d.). *Hike | Seven Falls | Tucson.* Arizona Hikers Guide. http://www.arizonahikersguide.com/all-hikes/hike-seven-falls-tucson

Sawyer, B. (2020, August 3). *Perfect Day Trip to Sedona - 12 Things to Do in Sedona.* Travel by Brit. https://www.travelbybrit.com/day-trip-to-sedona/#

Seven Falls in Tucson, Az. (2020, June 4). Epicplaces4u. https://epic-places4u.com/seven-falls-in-tucson-az/

Speakman, B. (2020, October 8). *Williams, Arizona; The Gateway to the Grand Canyon.* Travel thru History. http://www.travelthruhisto-ry.tv/williams-arizona/

Stevenson, T. (2022, January 19). *75 Best Arizona Quotes About The Beautiful Copper State.* The Travelling Tom. https://www.thetravellingtom.-com/arizona-quotes

Stewart, K. (2021, November 12). *The Perfect 1, 2 or 3 Days in Tucson Itinerary.* The World Was Here First. https://www.theworldwashere-first.com/tucson-itinerary/

Summerville, S. (2017, January 6). Buddhistdoor Global. https://www.bud-dhistdoor.net/features/where-peace-is-a-living-presence-the-stupa-peace-parks-of-kunzang-palyul-choling/

Tingom, J. (2023, January 28). *Catalina State Park With Kids.* Phoenix with Kids. https://www.phoenixwithkids.net/catalina-state-park-with-kids/

Topor, L. (2021, October 21). *The Jerome Grand Hotel Still Haunts This Old Ghost Town.* Thrillist. https://www.thrillist.com/travel/nation/jerome-grand-hotel-arizona-ghost-town

Travelingness. (2022, January 9). *7 Best Ways To Spend A Perfect Day In Tucson, Arizona.* Traveling Ness. https://www.travelingness.com/a-perfect-day-in-tucson-arizona/

Tucson Mountain Park. (n.d.). U.S. News. https://travel.usnews.com/Tucson_AZ/Things_To_Do/Tucson_Mountain_Park_65945/

Tucson Region (n.d.). Visittucson. https://www.visittucson.org/plan-your-visit/about-tucson/history/#:~:text=In%201877%2C%20Tucson%20was%20incorporated

Tucson, Arizona. (2023, March 20). Wikipedia. https://en.wikipedia.org/wiki/Tucson

Visiting Horseshoe Bend with Kids. (2022, April 15). Huddlebee. https://huddlebee.com/visiting-horseshoe-bend-with-kids/#:~:text=Horseshoe%20Bend%20is%20a%20stunning

Walk This Talk. (2020, July 10). Discover Flagstaff. https://www.flagstaffarizona.org/blog/walk-this-talk/

Walker, T. (n.d.). *Catalina State Park.* State Parks. https://stateparks.com/catalina_state_park_in_arizona.html

Walker, T. (n.d.). *Kaibab National Forest.* State Parks. https://www.stateparks.com/kaibab_national_forest_in_arizona.html

Weiser, K. (2022, September). *Jerome, Arizona – Copper Queen on the Hill – Legends of America.* Www.legendsofamerica.com. https://www.legendsofamerica.com/az-jerome/

Williams, L. (2022, September 8). *The Arizona Capitol Museum in Phoenix.* Lostinphoenix. https://lostinphoenix.com/arizona-capitol-museum-phoenix/

Wilsdon, J. (2022, May 22). *Museum of Northern AZ in Flagstaff: Unbeatable for Local History.* Wander Wisdom. https://wanderwisdom.com/travel-destinations/Museum-of-Northern-Arizona-in-Flagstaff-One-of-the-Best-Local-Attractions-and-Museums-of-History#gid=ci026e1f15d005245f&pid=museum-of-northern-arizona-in-flagstaff-one-of-the-best-local-attractions-and-museums-of-history-MTciMTExNjEzNzkwMTAyNjIz

Wittig, S. (n.d.). *Route 66 Attractions in Flagstaff, AZ.* Discover Flagstaff. https://www.flagstaffarizona.org/things-to-do/scenic-drives-day-trips/route-66/

Wupatki National Monument, Arizona, United States. Britannica. (2013, August 23). Www.britannica.com. https://www.britannica.com/place/Wupatki-National-Monument

Wupatki National Monument. (n.d.). Visit Arizona. https://www.visitarizona.com/places/parks-monuments/wupatki-national-monument/

Young, J. (2020, February 19). *Sycamore Falls: Northern Arizona's Best Kept Secret.* Simply Wander. https://justsimplywander.com/sycamore-falls/

Young, J. A. (n.d.). *Jerome Arizona, A thriving Arizona Ghost Town | History, Yesterday and Today.* Arizona-Leisure. https://www.arizona-leisure.com/a-short-story.html

Zhanna. (2022, January 3). *How to Visit Sycamore Falls, Arizona.* Roads and Destinations. https://www.roadsanddestinations.com/2022/01/03/how-to-visit-sycamore-falls-arizona/#:~:text=during%20this%20time.-